HOW TO MAKE ANYBODY LIKE YOU

HOW TO IMPROVE YOUR CONVERSATIONS, WIN FRIENDS, AND FORM ALLIANCES WITHOUT CHANGING WHO YOU ARE

JONATHAN GREEN

Edited by
ALICE FOGLIATA

Copyright © 2018 by Dragon God, Inc.

All rights reserved.

Simultaneously published in United States of America, the UK, India, Germany, France, Italy, Canada, Japan, Spain, and Brazil.

All rights reserved. No part of this book may be reproduced in any form or by any other electronic or mechanical means – except in the case of brief quotations embedded in articles or reviews –without written permission from its author.

Make Anyone Like You has provided the most accurate information possible. Many of the techniques used in this book are from personal experiences. The author shall not be held liable for any damages resulting from use of this book.

Paperback ISBN: 9781718081079

CONTENTS

Don't Go it Alone	v
1. You Spot a Celebrity	1
2. All Men Are Created Equal	11
3. Say Hello	17
4. Transition	27
5. Digging for Gold	32
6. Landmines	41
7. Give Value	49
8. Favors Are Muscle	60
9. Open Loops	72
10. Open the Lines of Communication	80
11. The Golden Rule	92
12. Unlock your Superpower – Good Vibes are the Ultimate Value	100
13. Easy Ways to Give Value	108
14. Practice Makes Perfect	121
Let's Soar Together	125
More Information	127
Found a Typo?	129
About the Author	131
Books by Jonathan Green	135
One Last Thing	139

DON'T GO IT ALONE

The hardest part of personal growth is going it alone. This is a book about developing social skills and communicating with other people.

We have put together an amazing group of people on the same journey as you who would LOVE to help you succeed.

Join something bigger than yourself where you can get the support, feedback, and guidance you need to achieve your desired success.

Please join my FREE, private Facebook group, filled with supportive people on the same path as you!

https://servenomaster.com/community

This is a great place to chat with me daily, share your experiences with the exercises and find a supportive group of people who are all on the same journey as you.

1

YOU SPOT A CELEBRITY

You're on an elevator in a hotel. You're at a bar in a city you've never been to before. You're on a cruise ship. Suddenly, you spot a celebrity.

It could be a famous actor, an amazing musician, or a powerhouse within your industry. If they give you the nod, they could double, triple, or even 10x your income, effectively exploding the growth of your business.

You have just thirty seconds to make something happen and transform your life. What do you do?

If you don't have a plan for that moment, you will fail. We often just assume that we'll figure it out when the time comes, but we usually end up letting ourselves down. Without preparation and strategy, these great moments can turn into great disappointments.

Luck is what happens when preparation meets opportunity. –
Seneca

In this book, I'm going to show you how to prepare for

these moments and how to maximize the odds of opportunity coming into your life.

When we meet that celebrity, we often make the mistake of falling into a broken or an improper pattern. If we have no strategy for these situations, we'll fall back onto a bad strategy without realizing it.

I live in the middle of nowhere, yet I run into at least two to three celebrities a year when I'm traveling. I always try to make each thirty-second interaction a success, but not all of them have worked out. Some of them were absolute failures, while some of them are still helping me to grow my business in a major way.

I'm going to share with you each of those different journeys so that you can see and understand what I did right and what I did wrong.

Be Without Intent

Before we can get into technique, we want to focus on mindset. If you say the right phrase but you have the wrong mindset, it will trigger someone's defensive mechanisms. They'll smell a rat, they'll feel like you're disingenuous, and they'll distance themselves from you as quickly as possible.

In some ways, not being yourself is worse than saying the wrong thing. If you have the right words but the wrong emotion, desire, or mindset, you will repel the people you most want to bring into your life.

This mindset goes far beyond just meeting celebrities. It applies to every interaction you have, whether it be in your personal, business, or social life. If you want someone to like you, it is critical that you have the correct mindset, which is to be without intent.

Do not have a hidden ulterior motive that you are just

waiting for the right moment to spring upon someone.

If you talk to someone while masking your ultimate goal, the person you're talking to will be able to tell that you have an underlying objective that's driving the conversation. They might not know what it is, but they will sense that you are hiding something. And it will repel them.

If you start talking to me, and all you want is free access to one of my expensive courses, I'll notice that we're not really talking about what you're thinking about. There will be a disconnect between the words you're saying and the thoughts you're thinking. The goal you're seeking will ultimately break the attraction between you and the person you're talking to, and the conversation will quickly go from magnetic to repellent.

When you approach a celebrity and pretend that you don't want an autograph when that's actually all you want, the conversation will be stilted. It's better to be honest and build that up as a clear direction for the interaction.

To be without intent means that you are *living in the moment*. Rather than thinking about a long-term goal, you're simply focused on having a great conversation.

If you can have amazing conversations and give people good experiences, all the other pieces will fall into place. You won't have to work so hard to reach your goal.

This process of reaching your goal by not working toward your goal may seem counter-intuitive, but it actually makes things easier. It will get you what you want, and it applies across the board.

Many a man will talk to a woman with the sole intent of getting her phone number. For the woman, the interaction feels fake. When a man walks up to a woman and starts talking to her about the weather, what's on television, and what's happening with other people in the room, but all he really wants is to get her phone number and take her on a date, the conversation becomes disingenuous – she knows he has an ulterior motive in the conversation. It almost feels like he's just saying enough words to get to the point where he can ask for her phone number.

Once he finally gets the number, he exits the conversation. He got what he wanted, so the conversation is complete for him, while the woman is left feeling almost used. When he finally calls the phone number, however, he's shocked when she doesn't answer.

We've all been through this experience, and it doesn't feel very nice. We don't like when someone talks to us just because they want something. Your conversations should be without intent to create genuinely nice feelings for yourself and your conversation partner.

It's easy for me to tell you to be without intent, but how can you actually do it? There are three ways that you can implement this mindset very quickly.

1. Stop Assuming

Your ulterior motive comes from a broken assumption, and that's where the flaw in conversation comes from.

In dating, the assumption is that you want to be with someone purely based on their looks. When you decide you are attracted to someone purely because of the way they look, it renders the conversation meaningless. This is the mistake that most people make. There are plenty of stunning people that you would never want to go on a date with.

It's the same for a business conversation. Before you assume that a celebrity is like their public persona or that a business leader would be great to work with, you need to get to know them.

I was once approached for a business deal by someone very successful in my industry. With a little research, I discovered that he had been fined nearly $50,000,000 by the FTC for false advertising. They contacted every single one of his customers and not one had a positive experience. Without a deeper look, I could have tread on some dangerous ground.

The core mindset in every conversation is, "I think this person is great – now I'm going to talk to them and find out if I'm correct." This changes the goal of your conversation from getting something from the other person to finding out if they are awesome.

2. Positive Vibes

The first is to focus on making sure that everyone you talk to has a good time. If the purpose of your conversation is to give the other person joy, and that is all you focus on, your conversations will be amazing and more people will like talking to you.

I'm not telling you to be servile and to become someone else's slave. Just focus on making your conversations enjoyable, and you will eventually find a good balance between a good conversation and not being a pushover.

You'll have to work your way through this process to find the right path for you. As you do, you'll find your conversations get better, and people will like talking to you more.

2. Mechanics of a Conversation

The second way to become without intent is to break a conversation down into pieces.

The very first book about social interactions that I wrote

was about the structure of a conversation built around flirtation. In that book, I break a romantic conversation into many tiny pieces from hello all the way to starting a relationship.

I spent a long time just learning how to say hello in a way that didn't instantly turn people off. Once I had mastered the hello, I then focused on mastering the transition from hello into a conversation.

After that, I focused on the part of the conversation called attraction. This is where you want to demonstrate to the other person that you are intriguing, interesting, and that you have something to offer them.

There are plenty of books that go into depth about how to master dating. This is not one of those books. This is a book about understanding that successful conversations can be broken into a replicable structure.

Every successful conversation can be broken into a script. Take a look at an infomercial, call the phone number, and see what happens. Everything they say is built on the same structure, regardless of what they're selling.

If you talk to a salesperson, they go through a structure where they take you through a series of emotions. There's a strategy to the conversation, and there's nothing wrong with this.

Remember, if your goal is to sell someone a product that is good for them and to make them feel good in general, then going through the correct structure is fine. When you have good sales techniques, people will recognize it and appreciate your professionalism.

There's nothing wrong with having a structure. People use them on me all the time. Every time I have a conversation with a salesperson who uses good sales techniques, I appreciate it because I recognize it as professionalism.

It's fine to have an ultimate goal, but you shouldn't leak or reveal that ulterior motive until you've gone through the beginning phases of a conversation.

Every time I talk to someone who can help my business, I don't focus on my ultimate goal until we've gone through the earlier phases of interaction. We need to get to know each other, see if we're on the same page, and see if we're in the same financial realm.

I recently had a conversation with someone who was looking for a ghostwriter. He was looking for someone at a much lower rate than me, and I understood that for what he was building, unfortunately, I wasn't the right ghostwriter for him.

We followed the correct structure of a conversation and found a solution that would help both of us in the long run. Although it did not lead to a sale for me, it led to the beginnings of what could be an amazing confluence between our two businesses.

When you follow the structure in the right order and focus on one step at a time, you will follow the path to success. When we do one thing but think about something else, our hidden intent will block any successful conversation from happening.

If you want to see this in action, I recommend the movie *Tao of Steve*. This is a movie about a fat guy with a dead-end job who smokes too much marijuana, works two days a week, and dates loads of beautiful women.

While I'm not in alignment with many of the principles in this movie, his demonstration and explanation of how to be without intent are excellent.

It comes from studying the writings of Buddha, so if you want to go one step further, you can read more about this religion and philosophy. The goal is to only think about what you're doing right now. Don't think about what this person can do for you. Instead, think about what you can do for them.

If you just focus on making every conversation a good experience for the other person, you will have mastered this chapter.

Reflection Questions

You're going to create a journal called the How to Make Anyone Like You Journal. You can take notes on your computer or your phone if you want to, but I find that using your hands and writing in a physical format brings you the most success.

I keep at least five notebooks with me all the time to track my projects, plan the future of my business, and outline books (including this one.)

You can go to the dollar store, the grocery store, or a bookstore and pick up any little fifty-cent notebook. Having a physical notebook is easiest for what we're trying to do. It will allow you to flip through the pages easily to find whichever bit of information you're looking for.

One of your first activities is to write down your answers to these questions in your Journal.

Take some time and be serious. The more time you invest thinking about your answers and being honest with yourself, the faster you'll find success from this book.

1. Have you ever been in a conversation with someone where you could tell that they wanted something from you? How did it make you feel? How did the conversation end? Maybe they wanted to date you, sell you something, or get

you to invest in something. Did you end up giving them what they wanted, or did that hidden motive repel you?

2. Think of a specific moment in your life when you wanted something from someone, and it didn't go right because they noticed that you had an ulterior motive. Look back at that conversation and write down what you could have done differently.

3. Why are you reading this book? What is your goal? What would you like to accomplish by the end of this book? Maybe you want to be able to have conversations with people of the same gender, with people of the opposite gender, or with potential business partners. Write down your goal and include a timeframe, whether it be thirty, ninety, or 180 days. "I would like to be able to reach this goal in that amount of time." Creating that nice, long-term goal will help you to stay on track and to measure your progress.

4. What does it mean to you to be without intent? Take the time to write more than just one sentence. Really dig into this phrase and see if it holds meaning within your heart.

5. What is your ideal conversation? Who is it with? Maybe it's with a celebrity, a business leader, or someone you've had a crush on since high school.

Write down at least a paragraph or two showing exactly how you see the interaction going. Start with hello and move from there. What comes next? How does it move from one topic to the other? Does it end with a job offer, with a phone number, or with a promotion?

Activity

You can't learn to have a good conversation without talking to other people, just like you can't learn to swim without getting in the water. Luckily, we can practice and master these skills without going too far outside your comfort zone.

Before you go to the next chapter, talk to ten strangers with the sole goal of making them feel good. If you remove all other goals, you will have no other hidden intent for the conversation.

For example, you can talk to someone attractive, but you're not allowed to ask for their phone number. You can talk to business people, but you're not allowed to give them your card. You could even go to job interviews and not ask for the job. When you create this rule, you have removed intent.

Work your way through ten people that you normally interact with but have never really talked to. It could be a cashier at the grocery store or the teller at the bank.

Maybe you've always thought of them as drones or part of the background of your life, but, for the next few days, you're going to talk to ten of them with the goal of giving each person you talk to a good feeling.

In each of these interactions, your only goal is to make the other person have an enjoyable conversation. That is the only goal. There is nothing else.

When you complete this activity, you'll have a firmer understanding of what it means to be without intent. The lesson of this chapter will be embedded in your mind, and then you'll be ready to join me in the next chapter.

2

ALL MEN ARE CREATED EQUAL

The first mindset we've covered that will help you achieve massive success is being without intent. The second mindset is one of the core tenants of the American politic: all people are created equal.

One of the most common mistakes people make when they approach someone they admire is to act like that person is better than them.

I'm a weird kind of famous. If you have read my books and follow my website, you know who I am. But if you haven't read my books and don't follow me, you've probably never heard of me.

Not everybody knows every celebrity. I've interacted with quite a few celebrities I had never even heard of. I have regular conversations based on my ignorance, and that's a critical lesson.

One time, I was at a VIP Club in England,[1] where you have to dress to the nines and spend way too much money just to get in. I started a conversation with the guy standing next to me at the bar. We had an amazing conversation and even threw back a few shots of tequila together. I discovered later that he played for England's national football team. If I had approached him like a fan, the conversation would have been very different.

You've probably heard about the Stanford prison experiment.[2] It's a well-known study from the seventies where they took a group of college kids and dressed half of them as prisoners and half of them as guards.

People started falling into the role very quickly. The guards were abusing the prisoners, and it had such an effect on the participants that this two-week experiment was ended after only seven days.

The lesson to take from this experiment is that people will fill the roles we put them into. If you act like a fan talking to a celebrity, that becomes the relationship dynamic. More often than not, it's the fan that creates this dynamic, not the celebrity.

This is a mistake that most men make when trying to talk to an attractive woman. They have this mindset that the woman is up on a pillar and they are beneath her. They feel like they have to do something to create equality.

When my business was teaching men how to talk to women, I saw a particular system in which the man would attempt to raise his own value by lowering hers. After about thirty minutes, the man would finally feel equal to the woman.

This is a terrible mistake, and if you avoid using it, you will have a massive advantage over anyone trapped in that flawed system. If you see yourself as equal to the person you are attracted to from the beginning, you will have a thirty-minute advantage over everyone else. Instead of trying to impress a girl because she's beautiful, you should simply see if your personalities are a good fit for each other.

If you look at interactions as two people looking for a

connection, all the stress disappears. You don't have to impress that beautiful woman, the celebrity, or the person interviewing you for a job. You're simply determining if your personalities click.

This book is not about making sure nobody ever hates you. There's always going to be someone who you just cannot connect with. Instead, this book is about maximizing the odds of having a great connection with everyone you talk to.

There will always be things outside your control, but, when you have success after success, the occasional falter doesn't become as significant.

The principle here is that *all people are equal*. You can meet a movie star and treat them like a movie star, but you shouldn't be surprised when they treat you like a fan instead of an equal.

Being a celebrity is a job, not your core identity. If you treat them like normal people who happen to work as actors or musicians, the interaction becomes much easier. It removes the pressure on you to try to impress them and equalize. Instead, you're just two people having a normal conversation.

It's refreshing for celebrities to be treated like normal people. There's a reason they go out in disguise all the time. Sometimes, they just want to have a normal interaction.

Instead of being like all the other fans, we want to be the exception to the rule. We want to have conversations that they don't have with other people. That's how you become memorable.

Reflection Questions

Please take the time to write down the answers to these questions in your Journal.

1. Have you ever had a conversation with someone where they treated you like a celebrity or a superstar? How did it make you feel when they put you on a pedestal? How did the conversation end? Did it turn into a friendship, or did they lock into that celebrity-fan dynamic?

2. If people treated you like you were defined by your career and nothing else, how would that make you feel? Would you enjoy that type of conversation? Does the idea of someone talking to you like an actual person with feelings make you feel better? Would you appreciate being treated like someone who is more than just your career?

3. Pick a particular person or type of interaction that you would like to maximize. It could be a beautiful woman, a movie star, a business leader, or something you worked on in the previous chapter. I want you to write down the interaction from that person's point of view.

What is the world like for them? What does it feel like for this person when everyone they talk to wants something from them? What does it feel like to be a celebrity when people are just waiting to see you make a mistake? What would it feel like to be under that microscope all the time?

I was once having a conversation with someone who's famous in my industry, and, during that conversation, ten different people interrupted us to pitch business ideas to him. This has become his entire world. Everyone has an idea to pitch to someone who is successful.

I would hate to live like that.

If we can empathize with other people's experience of the world, we can start to master the art of conversation. Once you understand someone else's experience, you can speak to them from a place of parity. Nobody wants to be treated like an object and this is how to break through it.

Activity

Your activity is to interview three people and find out what they hate about how people treat them. We're trying to understand how other people experience life so that we can form a sense of empathy.

You can go to your local bar and ask the bartender, "What's it like to have to listen to everyone talk about their problems? Does anyone ever ask you what your life is like? What does that feel like?"

You could ask a beautiful woman, "What's it like to know that men who talk to you are just waiting for the moment when they can ask you out? How does that feel?"

You can even make predictions. You can ask that beautiful woman, "Does it feel like most people just assume you're dumb because you're attractive? What does that feel like? Do people always assume you won't have a great personality just because you're nice looking?"

In Guardians of the Galaxy 2, Drax, the character played by the former professional wrestler Bautista says something quite brilliant. "Beautiful people never know who to trust."

I just want you to understand how other people experience life and how they feel about their interactions. Let's find out how accurate this quote is and try to develop some empathy here.

You can talk to your friends, people that you admire, or someone who has an extremely different lifestyle than you. Find out the characteristic that most people who approach them focus on.

Sometimes people approach me and all they want is business advice. They want me to look over their book ideas or even give them free access to one of my courses. This doesn't make for a very good interaction.

As you interview each person, they will have similar experiences. They don't like talking to selfish people who only want something from them. This builds on the lessons we've learned so far that if you're honest and genuine, the conversations will be powerful and effective.

It's now time to go out and interview at least three people or even more if you're feeling motivated. I want you to get confirmation from real people about what you're learning in this lesson. It's critical that you anchor the words from this book in reality through experience. When you've completed those interviews, you can join me in the next chapter.

[1] I used the techniques from this very book to get into clubs like this all the time in London. Since I was barely scratching a living at the time, I had to use social skills rather than money to gain access to these hoity-toity institutions.

[2] I'm aware that some participants have decided forty years later to claim that parts of the experiment were faked. Whether that's true or not, the principle is correct.

3

SAY HELLO

There are two main approaches to a conversation. You either have a strategy or you don't. Most of us are not tactically-minded, so we approach a conversation with no strategy. We just go up to someone, say whatever pops into our heads, and we see how things play out.

When you are in a conversation where a successful outcome matters to you, relying on luck is the worst possible strategy. Whether it's talking to an attractive person or someone you want to do business with, you want to minimize luck as a factor.

The larger part luck plays in your endeavors, the worse your life will be.

If you simply hope you'll say the right thing in the moment, you're always going to struggle. It's okay to believe that you'll think of something creative at that moment, but there is a time and a place for luck. It can't be your overall strategy.

We're now going to work through the phases of a conversation together, starting with the introduction, or saying hello.

For people who are very nervous and a little overwhelmed by the person they're talking to, hello feels like an insurmountable mountain. They stress over finding an opener[3] that is so brilliant that the person will immediately fall in love with them.

I've approached around 50,000 strangers, and only one person has ever remembered the first thing I said to them. I will often start a conversation with someone and later ask them, "Do you remember the first thing I said to you?"

They never do.

The mountain seems big until you're on the other side of it. Once you overcome the hello hurdle, it's no longer a big deal. Your hello only has to be more interesting than the fact that you walked over.

When people are first learning to talk to strangers, a common activity is to walk up to ten strangers and ask what time it is, where the bathrooms are, or what time the store closes. This is a fine exercise for beginners, but it's not a good exercise to transition into a real conversation.

You can use a weak opener, but then you have to make up for that with the second thing you say. When you use weak openers that are basically fixed conversational structures, you're giving yourself very limited room to have a good conversation.

For example, if you walk up and ask the time, they will tell you the time, and the conversation is over. Then, you'll have to say something even better for your second sentence to transition from asking for the time to a conversation.

Instead, we want to use strategic conversational starters.

One of the most powerful ways to start a conversation is

to walk up, say, "Hi, I'm Jonathan," and shake their hand. It is ingrained in people to reciprocate the handshake and the introduction. This method is very effective, but it can feel too easy.

I'm going to share with you three powerful ways to start conversations.

1. **Script.** A script is a memorized conversation starter. We rely on scripts for presentations and speeches so that what we say is written out in advance.

We can apply this same principle to conversations we're having face to face with someone. You can memorize five or ten phrases for each specific environment you find yourself in.

An example of a script in the dating world that you might be familiar is to walk up to someone and say, "Excuse me, who lies more, men or women?"[4] This is a fixed script in which the question is more interesting than the fact that you've walked up. That's why it's so effective.

We're trying to go beyond just the dating world. There are loads of scripts all over the internet that you can try for various situations. You can memorize five or ten for each situation, and you can test and tweak them until you find a couple that work for you.

I became an expert at inventing creative and effective stories that can create a series of emotions.

One of my favorite ways of starting the conversation is to walk up to a nice lady and say, "Excuse me, I know you're having a meeting with your friends, and I don't mean to intrude. But, I noticed that the dress you're wearing looks amazing. My sister's a fashion designer in New York, and she told me that, when I see people with good fashion, I should say something to encourage the world to be a more beautiful place."

This is a long conversation starter, but every single word in it is strategic. Each part of it plays a role.

When I say, "Excuse me, I noticed you're having a meeting," it is to demonstrate that I'm socially aware. I know that when two people are talking and you interrupt them, it can be considered rude. I use the word "meeting" because we are in a casual social setting, so it's a funny misuse of the word.

I then deliver the compliment, and everything after that serves a single purpose of eliminating any obligation that the person might feel.

Most people don't know how to give a compliment. They deliver their compliment, and then they expect a response. That's not a compliment. That is an obligation. They have created an unpleasant conversational structure because they're trying to force someone to do something.

I don't tell the lady her dress looks nice so that she will say something nice to me; I say it because I believe it. When I say something after the compliment, she can't respond immediately. I change the subject to my sister, not even giving her the option to respond to the compliment.

I have changed the subject so quickly that she can't even say "thank you" for the compliment. I've already told her that I didn't give her a compliment for her. I gave her the compliment because my sister told me to.

This is a complicated structure, but it's powerful. We can modify this type of structure to fit with anyone we talk to. If you meet someone you admire, for example, you could say something like, "Excuse me, I'm a huge fan of your work. You don't have to say anything back to me. I just think when people do amazing work, they should be told."

This structure is so powerful that it would even work on me even when I'm completely aware that's it's coming. If you met me and memorized this script, you could say, "Excuse me, Jonathan. I read your book on how to make anyone like you, and it changed my life. It was amazing, and I felt an obligation to let you know that your book worked."

By saying something after the compliment, you shut down my obligation reflex, and you can start a cool, genuine conversation.

The basic structure of this particular script is to acknowledge what the person is doing at that moment, give them a compliment, and then diffuse their opportunity to respond by justifying your compliment in a way that has nothing to do with them.

This conversation starter is powerful, and it accomplishes our initial goal of making people feel good.

A great activity that you can try to see the full effect of this starter is to use it, then leave the room. In doing this, you are clearly demonstrating that you have no intent. You're just trying to make someone's day. Whether you're saying this to businessmen, entertainers, or beautiful women, you're acting like a magical fairy waving their wand and making everyone's life a little better.

Our compliment lacks intent because our motivation is external. Instead of saying, "I like your dress because I want to sleep with you," you're saying, "I wanted to say something nice because someone in my life motivated me."

You can find thousands of other conversational starters online, but you don't need an arsenal. Just choose one that you can easily remember that matches the way you communicate with people. The more genuine the phrase feels, the easier it will be for you to deliver.

2. Situational starter. Start your conversation by reacting to what's happening around you at that moment.

Before I was married, I would often say to women, "Wow, it's really crowded in here." It was a simple and true statement that could get a conversation going.

If you practice your observation skills a little, you can build on it. "Wow, there are a lot of people in here with badges. Everyone's wearing the same color shirt."

Depending upon your personality, you can even get funnier and more creative. Sometimes when I go to conferences where everyone's wearing the same type of clothing, I say, "Wow, it looks like everyone got their clothes from the same photocopier, but no one told me. I wish I knew about that. I would have joined in."

Sometimes these work, and sometimes they don't. One time a girl tripped and fell on me, and I said, "Oh, the gravity has been broken in here all night." She didn't think it was funny. Another time, I was standing next to a beautiful woman, and two guys started fighting. I turned to her and said, "Are they fighting over you?" She loved it.

Another time, I was in line with a bunch of beautiful women. One of the girls sneezed, and I said, "Excuse me, do you have bird flu?" Her friends thought it was hilarious, and I had a great conversation with all of them.

You can make it as creative as you want, but staying simple is often enough. "Wow, it's really crowded. Everyone is dressed the same. Everyone is really loud." We don't have to be super complicated – the majority of my relationships have started with one of these three sentences.

We have conversation starters and structures for you to memorize to stop you from saying terrible things that crush your value. If you act like a fan, people will treat you like a fan. We want to avoid that happening.

There are other conversational structures that are more advanced and complicated where you observe the room and set things up so that the person will talk to you. But, we don't need to get too complicated with this.

As long as you don't say something horrible, any conversational starter will work. We can start with a compliment wrapped in a justification or just say something situational. These simple structures are how I start 99 percent of my conversations.

It's only when we create massive amounts of pressure to say the perfect thing that it all goes wrong. These two types of conversation starters are the simplest ways to avoid saying something value-crushing.

3. Ask if they're someone or say that they look like someone. "You look like so-and-so. Are you this famous musician? You look just like this guy on that show I love."

The key to this approach is transitioning. I'll cover transitioning in greater detail in the next chapter, but the transition for this approach is, "What is someone like you doing in a place like this?"

Last year, I was at a conference in Bangkok. I had a problem with my laptop battery, so I ended up at this random repair shop in the middle of nowhere. It was on the fifth floor of a building on a street with no sign.

While I'm waiting for them to repair my laptop, in walks a famous DJ from the UK. I said, "Excuse me, are you this DJ? What are you doing in a computer shop like this?"[5] We ended up having a nice, normal conversation because of the random circumstances that led us both to that repair shop.

Using this approach, you can have a normal conversation that has nothing to do with them being a celebrity.

Later on, we'll talk more about the conversation itself, but for now, you have three very good approaches to begin a conversation.

Reflection Questions

1. Can you think of a time when your conversation opener was absolutely abysmal? What went wrong? What was your mistake?

2. Write out your own conversational starter using the structure from this chapter. Wrap up a universal compliment that you can modify to fit the situation. "I love your dress. I love your scarf. I noticed your amazing fashion sense. I can tell that you were using a strategy when you put together your outfit." If you create a simple way of giving a compliment and then saying something afterward to remove their sense of obligation, you can create a powerful conversation starter.

3. Think of two to three situational conversation starters that you can use. A great way to come up to this is to think of the last five to ten times you saw someone but couldn't think of something to say. What's something simple that would have fit that situation? It could be as simple as, "I love open bars. I love weddings."

4. Now that you are beginning to see that a conversation can have structure, are you starting to feel a little bit less intimidated about talking to strangers? Do you feel more hope and

excitement for the future? Do you think that this process could work for you?

Activity

In order to master the art of conversation, we have to practice talking to people. There are some very specific rules about how I want you to practice.

I do not want you to practice in a high-risk situation. Don't practice the techniques from this book for the very first time on the person that could change your life. You don't need to go all in.

Instead, find social situations where there are no consequences. You can go to Meetup.com and find groups that are focused on something that doesn't really interest you. You can go to a bar that's more than thirty minutes from your house. You can go to any event outside of your home city.

Find situations with people that you would never see again. This will let you make mistakes that you can learn from. You can tell jokes that don't quite hit, and it doesn't matter, as there are no long-term social consequences.

The more you practice in social settings that aren't connected to you, the more comfortable you'll feel using these techniques. You can say stupid things and not lose your job, or you can tell a joke that doesn't land and not lose out on a great networking contact.

Then, you can begin using it in your own environment. Eventually, you'll get to the point where you can use it on a stranger, and it works every single time.

For now, your activity is to go outside of your environment where there are no social or long-term consequences. Practice these different types of conversational starters without intent. Your goal is to talk to ten people, have a one-minute conversation, and then leave.

You can start a conversation with hello, a compliment, or simply introducing yourself. Talk with the person for no longer than sixty seconds. By forcing and mandating an exit, we guarantee that you are without intent.

This is a powerful teaching technique because it lets you see what it is like to have a conversation without intent.

This exercise is worth repeating until you master it. You should keep experimenting until you feel comfortable saying hello.

Whatever social environment you want to master, the structure for this exercise is universal. Repeat this exercise until you feel comfortable starting conversations. Feel what it's like to be without intent and have a little bit of structure and strategy. When you're comfortable with this, I'll meet you in the next chapter.

[3] An opener is a conversation starter – anything you use to "open" a conversation.

[4] This opener is memorialized in *The New York Times* bestseller *The Game* by Neil Strauss.

[5] To find out which DJ I met and how the story ended, head over to my blog at ServeNoMaster.com. I even have pictures.

4
TRANSITION

After you've mastered the art of "hello," it's very common to get frozen at what to say next. This step is called the transition. It is when you transition from a stranger to a conversation partner.

One of the reasons I didn't teach you some of the more complicated conversational starters is that they can lead to long conversations, and these can be a curse.

In the last chapter, I taught you some simple conversational starters. I mentioned one starter from the dating world. "Who lies more, men or women?" This starter will lead to a thirty-minute conversation. That may feel like a win to someone who is new to learning conversational structure, but, if you were to run into those people a week later, they wouldn't remember you.

Our mental filing system uses an algorithm to prioritize and sort the things we remember and the things we erase.

Single-topic conversations with a stranger are always deleted.

While you feel like you had a great conversation with all these different nuances, you've already been erased from their memory. This can happen in any setting from business to dating, and it's devastating. You feel like you put in all this work, and you thought the conversation went swimmingly, but you discover that you were unmemorable.

We must transition into a second topic of conversation so that we become a three-dimensional person in the movie of this person's day.

There are complicated transitional structures available, but the easiest way to transition is to simply change the topic. You can do this by stacking onto the first thing you said and following a social observation with the second one. "It's really crowded here. I love that there's an open bar. That's probably why it's so crowded."

These three sentences are all it takes. The first conversation was about crowd size, and the second is about open bars.

There's a direct correlation between the strength of a conversational starter and the necessary transition to maintain momentum. If you start with a weak conversational starter, such as, "Do you have the time?", you have to use a much stronger transition to make up for that.

Asking for directions and trying to turn that into a real conversation is hard to do because it seems like you were masking an intent. It's better to use one of the strong openers that I shared with you.

One of my favorite transition techniques is the observation. This is similar to the situational conversational starter, but it is more specific. An example of this would be to say, "Cool gloves!" First, you make a statement about the room. Then, you make a statement about the person.

When we use our stronger conversational starters, we

can accomplish a lot with a soft transition. Because the opener was so strong, the transition doesn't have to be. You could bring up any second topic.

In the previous chapter, I already mentioned one transition. "What's a person like you doing in a place like this?" You simply specify the person and the place. "What's a movie star like you doing in a wedding like this?" It's a simple yet powerful transition because it allows the person to talk about themselves.

A common mistake that people make is to talk to a movie star about their movies. For them, it's boring because that's what everyone talks to them about.

Instead, if you talk to a movie star about how they go to the same daycare as your kids, you'll have a better and more memorable conversation. If you find their primary motivation or something going on in their life that has nothing to do with their career, you'll stand out from all the other fans that approach them.

Transitions may seem intimidating, but they're actually very simple. The stronger your first sentence, the more you can get away with in the second sentence. As long as you start with a decent conversational starter, a simple secondary observation or subject change will suffice.

Reflection Questions

1. Have you ever had a conversation with somebody and you ran out of things to say? Why do you think that happened?

2. Which of these transitions feel most natural for you? Can you see it happening in a normal conversation? Have you used one of these before?

3. Can you devise a transition to attach to each of the conversational starters you developed in the previous reflection questions to have a two-sentence conversational starter stack?

4. Have you ever had a one-topic conversation with somebody? Do you remember the person or what you talked about?

Transition Activity

We're going to build on our previous activity. You should have already found an environment in which you can practice your techniques without social consequences. Your goal now is to go into this environment and have a two-part conversation.

Say hello, then transition.

You can stay in this phase as long as it takes to get comfortable going into the second part of the conversation. It may take you a single night, or it may take a few tries. That's okay. This is a process. Mastering the art of conversation and conversational structures can take a little bit of time because we're unlearning our bad habits and relearning better ones.

It is worthwhile to journal about your experience in this process. If the transition you're using doesn't work or you think of something creative, write it down.

When I was in this process, I became successful because I wrote blog posts about my efforts. My natural desire was to mumble and say boring things, but writing everything down helped me to become a successful conversationalist.

This exercise is very similar to the activity of the previous lesson. All we're doing is building on it. We want to build on these techniques to help you feel comfortable when the situation really matters. When you go in for a job interview or a big meeting with a potential investor, you already know what it feels like to say the right things.

Instead of going into a real environment, you want to stay in a practice environment. It will give you the practice and experience that you need to master a job interview or a meeting with a big investor.

Just as you don't want to read a book on swimming and then jump in the deep-end of the pool without having practiced in the shallow end, you should practice these techniques in the shallow-end of your social settings.

Practice your transitions. See what it's like to move a conversation forward to become three-dimensional. When you feel good about your transitions, then you can join me in the next chapter.

5

DIGGING FOR GOLD

Once we get past the opener and the transition, we're now in the part of the conversation where we can make people like you. This is the magnetic or attraction phase, which is where you draw someone to you.

This isn't necessarily an attraction in the dating sense. It's simply the moment where you can make people genuinely like you to form stronger connections.

Most men who are trying to meet women at a bar fear that, when they start talking to her, her husband or boyfriend will show up. He'll be using some technique or strategy, and, suddenly, her husband walks out of the bathroom.

She will introduce the man as her husband, and the guy slinks his head in shame, tucks his tail between his legs, and walks away feeling like a worm.

When you have strong conversational skills and understand how the attraction phase works, this will never happen to you again.

If I'm talking to a woman and her husband walks up,

there's almost a guarantee that he will buy me a drink within the next five minutes. Instead of slinking away, I immediately transition to the attraction phase with him. I say, "I didn't realize she was married. I would never disrespect you or your wife. What brings someone like you to a place like this?"

Instead of acting like a fox trying to break into someone's henhouse, I'm honest. This way, I am able to avoid any awkwardness or accusations.

I then go into the attraction phase with him. The attraction phase works on men or women in any situation. The idea here is to create someone who's engaged in the conversation.

Most often when I enter this phase with the husband, he is so engaged that the woman wonders why neither of us is talking to her. That's how powerful the magnetic phase is. The person on the outside disappears, and they want to be part of it.

There are three pillars of attraction: passion, honesty, and self-confidence. Depending upon the environment, you'll build on these more or less. In the dating world, for example, they need to be very strong, while, in the business world, you only need a slight demonstration.

Passion is particularly amazing. When someone talks about their passions, people are drawn to them. If you talk to someone about something you're passionate about, they'll immediately like you a little more. Plus, it makes for good conversation, and it never gets boring.

My general approach for everyone I meet is to dig for gold. I want to find something amazing about them. Depending upon the depth of relationship I'm seeking, I dig for gold in slightly different ways.

The softest way to dig for gold is called job collecting. I

use this when I'm not trying to actively form a long-term relationship, and I just want to have a nice, short-term conversation. This is a great way to talk to the friend of the person you are trying to connect with.

When I collect their job, I simply ask them what they do for a living. I ask a few critical, passionate questions about their job, and I show real interest in what they're saying.

My goal is to meet one person with every single job that exists. Every time I meet someone with a job I haven't seen before, I ask them to tell me something most people don't know about it. I want to learn just one insider secret.

I ask them, "What is something that most people don't know about your job? What's the weirdest thing about your job?"

This is a powerful technique because it makes the person feel like a star. I am interested in their career while most people aren't. I am making someone feel special. Remember, we want to make other people feel good. I don't have a secondary goal beyond making them feel good.

Most people treat blue-collar careers like garbage and look down on them. When I approach people and take a genuine interest in their job, it's important to them because I took the time to dig into what they do for a living.

When they find out that I am mildly famous, it means even more to them. I'm barely a D-list celebrity, but when I say I'm an author, people get excited. When they find out that I'm "more important" than they are, it means a lot to them, and they feel important for five minutes.

My entire goal is just to make people feel good. My conversational structures are developed to achieve that goal.

If you meet someone with a profession that you've already seen before, you can share your insight or knowledge that the previous person taught you about that job.

Most professions have special lingo. Waiters have certain terms that they use for people that don't tip. When I worked on an ambulance, we had a lot of slang terms that we used. When you work in a profession where you face death every day, you see some horrible things. The way we would deal with it was macabre humor.

Each profession has its own language that only fit within that group. It is a way of identifying themselves and creating a sense of shared existence.

This is one of the few times I get to use my Master's in Applied Linguistics in one of my books. Subgroups create ways of identifying themselves as a group. This is why they develop uniforms and language as a sense of shared identity.

If you look at high schools, every subgroup looks alike. They may say they want to be different, but the jocks look like the jocks, the punks look like the punks, and the nerds look like the nerds. They have their own style and way of speaking, and that's how people identify them.

When you meet someone in a profession, learn some of their secret language. The second time you meet someone in that profession, you can bring it up and demonstrate the knowledge you've captured.

You could say, "I met someone who does this, too. They told me..." This allows you to build a sense of rapport or connection with that person. They will feel like you understand them, even if you're not a part of their group.

This works for people that you're trying to form a soft connection with. These are the people that you'll probably only meet once, but it also works on your friends or people you want to do business with. Because it's such a soft technique, it's versatile. You could use it for the people you are practicing with, someone your friend works with, someone you're friends with, or even someone you want to do business with.

We can also use stronger techniques to dig for bigger pieces of gold. You can ask questions like, "If you never had to work again, what would you spend the rest of your life doing?" or "What's your favorite think about yourself?" Instead of finding out what someone does all the time, we are asking how they define themselves - you're now trying to find out how they see their best selves.

Some questions feel a little too personal, such as, "What is your favorite thing about yourself?" Many people would feel uncomfortable with this question, and it's hard to build up enough of a rapport in that short period of time to make them comfortable enough to answer.

But, if you couch it in other, softer terms, you can get the answer without making them so uncomfortable. "What do you love to do? What's your favorite way to spend your time? What do you love about the town where you grew up? What do you love about your profession? What do you love about your life?"

Often, people will want you to go first. They may feel it's a little too personal for that moment, so they want you to open up first. Luckily, it doesn't matter who goes first. Remember, if you talk about your passion, it's still magnetic.

I lead all the time. My answer changes a lot because my passions are always changing. Sometimes I'm passionate about surfing, other times I'm passionate about traveling, and sometimes I'm passionate about playing the guitar. These days, my passion tends to revolve around my children.

It's good to have an answer to the question before you ask it. If you have nothing to say when they ask you the question back, your conversation is going to go right off a cliff.

When you ask these questions, people say amazing things, but sometimes people will throw up a shield.

One time, I was talking to a beautiful woman that worked as an exotic dancer. I told her that I didn't want to talk about her work but rather what her passions were. Most men would love to hear a dancer talk about dancing. To me, that's extremely boring, and I know that it would have locked me into the dancer-customer dynamic that I wanted to avoid.

She began to tell me about her passion as an artist. She told me that to have a gallery show in London, you need to have a certain number of paintings. She was only two paintings away from being ready to display her art in a gallery in London. That was an interesting conversation about her passion and far more meaningful than a discussion about her particular career.

Sometimes, you have to dig one level deeper to get to their real passions. It's worth it to put in the effort to get to that unique conversation that they don't have with everyone else.

Using the three pillars of attraction – passion, self-confidence, and honesty – is so powerful because it gets you some amazing and unexpected conversations.

We'll talk about this later in the book, but having unexpected conversations is powerful. It's worth it to find out what's unique about someone because this gets you those amazing, passionate conversations.

If someone asks you about your passion and you answer it honestly and reveal something personal about yourself, you're capturing all three pillars in a single sentence. You were honest about something you're passionate about and you had the self-confidence to reveal it.

So often, we have garbage conversations with strangers. We never really connect on a personal level and spend most of the conversation talking about things that don't matter. These techniques I've given you can help you avoid those types of conversations.

We've now covered the two ends of the spectrum: collecting jobs and asking about someone's deepest passion. You have to find the correct calibration for you and for the different conversations you find yourself in.

You can't use the same structure for all situations. Sometimes, one structure is the right answer, but, sometimes, another is better. You have to assess your situation, as well as how you look, how old you are, your gender, and your personality.

While these structures are universal, you'll find that some things work better for you than others.

Some of these structures don't work for certain people. The flirtatious lines that I used in my single days wouldn't work for men that were better looking than me. If you're too good-looking, too smart, or too eloquent, those specific lines won't work.

Through experimentation, you can find the right tweak to these conversational tools to find the perfect tools for you. As you practice, you'll see that everyone likes these conversations that make them feel special and important.

By giving you a spectrum, you can experiment to find the right one for you. It doesn't matter which structure you use, as long as the conversation makes your conversation partner feel special and important.

Reflection Questions

1. What's your favorite thing about yourself?

2. What's your favorite thing about where you grew up?

3. What's your favorite thing about your job?

4. If you never had to work again, what would you spend all your time doing?

5. How do you feel when someone is actually interested in you on a core level? How do you feel when someone asks about the things that matter to you?

6. How do you feel now that you understand this conversational structure? Do you believe that you can now have a deep conversation within five minutes of meeting someone?

Activity

We're going to continue building on our previous activities by figuring out your calibration.

Long ago, I had a student who struggled with some of the conversational structures that I use because he was too good-looking. My mother met him once, and she even asked what I could teach him because he was so much better-looking than I was. It took him a while to find the right calibration that worked for him, but he eventually found that sweet spot.

I've worked with people who are smarter, taller, better looking than me, and better in business than me.

For this activity, you're going to continue experimenting in no-consequence environments to find your calibration. Find the questions that work for you using the three pillars of attraction.

Experiment in different environments with the two methods I've taught you: job collecting and asking about their deepest passions. Find what works for you in different situations and see how people react.

Ask your questions in different ways from the soft end and from the hard end of the spectrum. Experiment with how you phrase your questions. Say something gentle, then say something strong. See how people react to find the best way for you.

The more you experiment, the faster you'll find success. Continue to track your results in your Journal. The more you write down your results, the easier it will be to see what works and what doesn't, and the faster you'll find that epic success that you deserve.

6

LANDMINES

There are certain conversational mistakes that we want to avoid so you don't lose all the progress you've made. Some of them you may have heard about before, like don't talk about politics or religion, while some of them are particular to the conversation you're having.

I once saw a man trying to flirt with a woman, and he started talking about natural disasters. He asked her if she had lost anyone in one before, and, as soon as she said yes, you could hear the landmine click, and you knew the conversation was over.

He was obviously expecting her to say no, but she threw him a curveball. Never in a million years would he be able to resurrect the conversation and get back into the attraction phase after bringing up such an abysmal memory.

This is a conversational landmine. There's an old adage for lawyers that says, "Never ask a question you don't know the answer to." This is a perfect application.

Never ask questions where the answer might be a

landmine that could destroy the conversation and drive you off-track.

This is a surprisingly common mistake because we tend to ask questions without realizing what the answer might be. It's important to think about all the possible answers, not just the most likely or preferred answer. You have to cover all your bases. Don't just hope that everything is going to go your way.

In today's world, talking about politics is a terrible way to form a connection with someone. It is such a divisive path that could derail the entire conversation. Don't assume that just because someone is on the same financial path as you that they share your political or religious beliefs.

There's no reason to bring up these topics. If you're somebody who is driven by divisive topics, you'll never make everyone like you. These people only surround themselves with others who agree with them, and they end up in a state of groupthink. That's not the path you want to go down.

Instead, focus on carefully avoiding unnecessary conversational mistakes. You're looking to form bonds with people who have a specific set of desirable assets. Whether your goal is to form connections with friends or business associates, you must stay in alignment with your goal, and bringing up divisive topics will not help you do that.

Avoid Their Strength

The second conversational mistake is to focus on someone's greatest area of strength. This isn't necessarily a full-on landmine, but it can easily become one. When people have a lot of something, it becomes what they are least interested in, and it becomes the lowest value you can offer them.

If you approach a billionaire and offer them a dollar, they're not going to be interested in it. It's a low value to them because they already have a billion of them.

If you offer someone a menu after they have just finished eating at a restaurant, they're not going to be interested. When people have a lot of something, that something becomes the last thing you should talk about with them.

If someone has zero dollars and you give them one dollar, that is a huge value to them because you have increased their value by 100 percent.[6] While your value could be high for this person, one dollar wouldn't be a high relative value for someone who already has a billion of them.

You need to pay attention to the people you're talking to and build your conversation around something other than their area of greatest strength. For them, it's not very valuable, and it's the most common conversational thread that they come across.

I was once on a cruise ship talking to one of the leaders in my industry, and our conversation was interrupted ten times by people trying to pitch ideas to him. It was disrespectful to him, and all they were doing was pitching business ideas to him.

The first time someone interrupted with a business idea, I thought it was pretty interesting. But by the tenth time, I began to realize how much he must hate it.

Our conversation, however, was about my strength and about a project I was working on. I was talking about my passion in a niche that he didn't have a presence in. I wasn't pitching to him, but by the end of it, he asked to partner with me on a project.

Instead of me pitching to him, I talked about my passions and the value I have that he didn't have. In the end, he was pitching to me.

He saw my passion and strength in an area where he wasn't strong. He saw opportunity whereas everyone else was busy offering him a strength he already had.

All of these people were making the mistake we'll talk about in the next chapter, which is to not give value but to try and take it. They saw a captive audience and an opportunity to throw their life raft at this larger boat in the hopes of being dragged along on the path to success. It never works when you do that.

The areas where people are strong are usually where they get the most offers, which is of little value to them.

I get so many emails from people offering to edit my books. It's not a value that I need because I already have a full-time editor who understands my voice and is able to match my pace of content creation.

For some authors, when someone offers to do your editing, it feels like an offer wrapped around an insult. It's almost like saying, "Your book has bad editing. Let me fix it for you." I can understand the desire to reach out to your author and give value, but it's not a value that all authors need.

When people send me that email reaching out where I'm already strong, I don't pay a lot of attention. Before I had my current editor, it was definitely something that would have peaked my interest. But now, I ignore most of these emails.

The emails that get my attention are about things where I am weak, like programming or designing board games.[7] When people send me a list of things that they're strong at, it often turns into a future project together.

Don't Have the Same Conversation

The most important lesson to take away from this chapter is to *not* have the same conversation with someone that they've had with hundreds of other people. When you repeat what everyone else does, it's very hard to keep someone's interest.

If you watch any successful person for ten minutes, you can figure out what conversation they have all the time.

Beautiful women hear, "You're so beautiful," all the time, and the men who say it can't figure out why they get terrible reactions. It's not that she's pretentious or thinks she's better than him. It's that she's had the same conversation a million times, and it's no longer interesting.

When you repeat what the crowd is doing, it's hard to be interesting.

Having the same conversation a thousand times is not interesting. Even if it was at one time interesting, it loses its appeal after the tenth time having the same conversation.

Think about your favorite food. Imagine eating that and only that three times a day for the rest of your life. Suddenly, something that used to be amazing is now horrible.

As you're designing your conversational structures, it's very important in this phase not to fall into the mistake of bringing up a divisive topic, asking a dangerous question, or focusing on where your conversation partner is strong.

We want to offer value from other parts of our personality. We don't want to repeat the conversations they've had with everyone else.

When you are the exception, you become a stronger memory. You become someone they want to talk to again because you're not just like everyone else.

The person who walks up to the celebrity and asks for an autograph will get that autograph, but that's all they will get. If you act like a fan, you'll lock yourself in the fan position, and you'll never be able to transition into a friend.

Reflection Questions

1. Have you ever said something that killed the conversation? Have you ever stepped on a conversational landmine? Write down what went wrong, what your mistake was, and how you can avoid doing it again.

2. Have you ever been in a conversation that you enjoyed, but then the other person said something that completely turned you off from talking to them? Can you remember what the landmine was? What question did they ask that ruined everything? Did they bring up a forbidden topic?

3. To prepare for conversations with the types of people you want to attract in your life, we need to make a list of the ten areas where you're the strongest. Think of the areas where you have the most knowledge, strength, experience, or skill. If you meet someone who is strong in five of your areas, you know five areas to avoid and five areas that you can talk about.

Even within your areas of strength, you sometimes have to subdivide into smaller sections. Look at your areas of strength and subdivide it them if you can. We're going to use this list as an asset later on.

4. Look back at some specific conversations with people you wanted to bond with where something went wrong. Was your mistake falling on a landmine, or were you just having a boring or repetitive conversation? Were you focused on an area where they were already strong?

Activity

For this activity, we're going to learn about conversational landmines, and reality television shows are a great place to start. If you watch some investing or dating reality television shows, you'll see that it's surprisingly easy to make everything go awry with one landmine.

On these shows, every time someone steps on a conversational landmine, they'll pause the show and highlight it, drawing attention to that mistake. They often mask when things are going right, but they always show when things are going wrong.

They might be looking for an investment or want to go on a date, and it looks like they're about to have a great success. Then, suddenly, they say the one thing that ruins everything. They let something slip out, and it turned interest into disinterest.

In your Journal, create a list of common landmines for your type of conversation, whether it be for dating, friendship, or business conversations.

I encourage you to go out and continue experimenting in no-risk situations. Listen to other people having conversations and look for the landmines. When you spot one, write it down.

Anytime you find a new landmine that fits your worldview, write it down so you can learn from other's mistakes as well as your own.

Just remember that landmines are not universal. Sometimes you can say something in one situation but not another. Certain conversations are acceptable. If you're fat, you can say certain things that skinny people can't get away with saying. If you're tall, you can say things that short people can't say. We have to continue to build on our structure based on our unique, individual properties.

Go out into the world and continue to build on your experiments. We are trying to be magnetic, but, if something goes wrong, learn from your mistakes. When you've begun to build this list and have a deeper understanding of landmines and conversational mistakes to avoid, you'll be ready to join me in the next chapter.

[6] I know that this isn't technically true, but you have increased their wealth by one hundred cents – which I think is a very lovely pun!

[7] I'm no longer weak in board games because someone emailed me about them, and we built my first game together!

7
GIVE VALUE

In the previous lesson, we talked about avoiding other people's strengths and, instead, focusing on your own. In this chapter, we're going to build on that by giving value.

There are two types of people in this world: those who want to take and those who want to give. If we can get into the mindset of being a giver, you will find great conversational success.

Most big conversational mistakes come from being a taker, and it often happens because we're caught by surprise. A lack of preparation causes us to react in an emotional way. When we think this is our one shot at success, our natural instinct is to just take it before it vanishes.

Let's look at an example. You're standing in an elevator when the CEO of your company gets on with you. This is a person who, with a single word, could double or triple your income, put you in charge of a massive sector, or give you a huge promotion. You get caught in the moment and ask,

"Could you give me one tip about what I could do to be a good CEO like you?"

Or perhaps you're at a conference, and you see a speaker that you're a huge fan of. You end up sitting next to him at the bar. You think, "This guy just spoke to a room of 5,000 people, and I get some one-on-one time with him. This is my one chance. I better think of something really smart to say. Let me get the best value I can." So you say, "Hey, let me ask you my biggest question."

Or a model, a movie star, or a rock star walks into the room. You're so thrown by meeting this person, and you haven't prepared, and you end up stuttering out a demand for too much value.

It's our natural inclination, when we think a resource is diminishing, to grab as much as we can.

When people ask their biggest question to virtual strangers, they fall into the pattern of being a taker.

Let's say you meet a beautiful supermodel. You ask her, "How can a guy like me date a girl like you? Give me some advice." These women get asked this question all the time, and it is people taking value from them.

We have this belief that favors are zero-sum. People think that if they do too many favors, they'll run out, or if I do a favor, you have to do a favor for me before I'll do another favor. We get caught up counting and tracking favors, and it leads us down a path that's a waste of energy. It's far better to simply give as much value as possible.

What Does it Mean to Give Value?

Giving value is simply focusing on giving something to another person. What can you do to help them? How can you help them have a good time? How can you help them grow?

There are some easy ways to give value, but you have to understand your social environment to figure out which one to use.

Almost nobody buys men drinks, so when you do, it feels special to him. I can tell you this as a man myself.

If you want to buy an hour of my time, you would have to approach me a customer, and it would cost $500. It used to be only $100, but, as I've gained experience, the price has gone up.

However, if you see me at a conference, you could buy me a drink at the bar, and that would earn you enough goodwill to get twenty or thirty minutes of my time. All you would have to do is say, "Hi, I'm a big fan. Can I buy you a drink?"[8]

This was one of the main ways that I grew my business. I found people I wanted to do business with and bought them drinks. It's a very easy way to give value, and it's not expensive at all.

If the person you want to give value to doesn't drink alcohol, buy them a dessert. I once saw someone do this. They said, "I'm a big fan. I know you don't drink. Can I buy you a slice of cheesecake?" It's a simple and easy way to give value. And it demonstrated they had researched the person and respected their life choices.

Remember, we don't want to give value where other people are strong. People who skipped the Landmines chapter, will walk up to a beautiful woman and give her ten compliments about her looks. That's where she's already strong.

Instead, give her compliments about her intelligence, her opinion, her conversational skills, or her fashion sense. We want to give people value in new ways.

You could approach a business person who's written a book or made a product that you bought and liked, and you could offer to film a thirty-second promotional video for the product.

You could say, "Your product was amazing and really helped transform my life. Can I shoot a video for you? We stand next to each other and I just say how great your product is. You could use it in your commercials or on your website." That's a massive value for people in business.

Not every one of these techniques works on every person. Depending upon how successful a person is, the things that are valuable to them will change. Someone who has a smaller business would love a promotional video. But, if someone's selling 10,000 units a day, they have so many reviews coming in that a promotional video is a pretty common resource for them.[9]

How often they get something will affect the value. They're still going to appreciate it, but it might not be a huge value to them. As you approach people that are more successful, we have to adjust our approach again.

Value in the Moment

Another way to give value is to give situational value. At any given time, someone is focused on a particular result. There is a primary thought in their mind about something they're working on in their business or personal life.

When your children are three or four years old, you start

to focus on where you're going to send them to school. You visit potential schools, do interviews, and meet with principals and admissions experts. It can be overwhelming to try to find the right school for your child.

If the billionaire you want to talk to is going through this process, and if you have a child going to one of the schools they're looking at, you have now become valuable to them. You have insight and knowledge that they don't have, and you could offer to give them that information.

If you overhear this person talking about how they're looking for schools for their kids, you could say, "My kids go there. I'd love to tell you what my experience has been." Most people would say yes because that's extremely valuable.

It's important to understand that this information has a value arc. As the person goes through the decision-making process, your information is valuable. But, once they've made that decision, your information is worthless. Once they've chosen a school, they are no longer looking for information about this topic. They've moved on to seek a new value.

Last year, I was trying to find longboard surfboards and standup paddleboards. At that time, this was the value I was seeking. Every day, I was constantly checking online groups, and anyone who had what I wanted became a high value for me. Any email about a longboard or standup paddleboard would have gotten my attention.

Now that I've completed my longboard collection, information about them is no longer valuable to me. If you send me an email about longboards, it wouldn't get my attention as much as it would have when it was a value I was seeking. I still check every once in a while just out of curiosity, but I've moved on to seeking a new value.

You have to strike while the iron is hot. When we talked about the transition, "What's a person like you doing in a place like this?", that question is really, "What value are you seeking right now?"

You can see the value that people are seeking anytime they do an interview because it's the thing that they are promoting. "This is my new book. This is my new album." They're trying to sell copies of it. It might not be the highest value they're seeking personally, but it's their highest professional value at that time.

This is a learning process, and there's a learning curve to it. You're going to make mistakes, and that's okay. You don't have to always guess right. This is more about switching to the correct mindset than it is always guessing the correct value.

What if People Take Advantage of Me?

You might be afraid that you'll continuously give value without ever getting anything in return. People who only take but never give do exist, and you'll probably run into them every once in a while. The good news is that Karma always gets them.

You could track and count the favors you do to make sure you get all your favors back, but I don't recommend it. There's no reason to be a hyper-tracker because your value will always come back to you one way or another.

I never pay attention to the number of favors I do for people because I see it as farming. Sometimes people take advantage of me because I'm not paying attention, but I'm putting good Karma into the world by giving as much value as possible, and it always comes back to me tenfold.

If I give person A a ton of value and they never return it,

I don't worry about it because I know it will come back to me through person B. You could spend your time tracking, and you'll know right away that person A hasn't returned your favor. But the cost in the long run is high, and it's not worth it.

You should always approach life by thinking, "How can I give someone value today?" Value doesn't necessarily mean financial value. You don't need to give someone a gold coin to give them value. You don't have to be on par with someone financially to help them.

Sometimes it's enough to make someone feel good when they're having a tough moment. A little bit of help, kindness, and grace can go a long way.

When you approach people with the mindset of giving value – whether it be kindness, advice, or knowledge – you'll find that you get an amazing return on your investment.

I mentioned a few chapters ago that famous DJ I met in a random computer shop in Thailand. He was there because his computer was broken, and he had a concert that night. I offered to lend him a computer so he could perform his show, saying, "People from out of town need to stick together."

He ended up not needing my computer, but my simple offer of kindness turned into a conversation, which led to him finding out that I'm a ghostwriter and us exchanging email addresses.

Unfortunately, it never went past a few emails.

Not every interaction I have knocks one out of the park. Sometimes it's not the right fit. Perhaps, down the line when he has an idea for another book or has a friend who needs a ghostwriter, something will come of this interaction. But for now, we're just planting the seeds.

I started from a place of giving value, and the conversation was very easy. Instead of walking up as a fan and asking for a photo or an autograph, I gave him value. We did end up taking a picture together, and it's on my website if you want to see it. But by giving him value first, I was able to avoid being just another forgettable fan.

Every new interaction is an opportunity to give value, even if you just make someone feel good. When we focus on giving value, people want to be around us. We become magnetic, and everyone starts rooting for us to succeed.

Reflection Questions

1. Think about who you want to interact with. In which areas are they already strong?

2. In which areas where you are uniquely strong? What value can you offer to people that will separate you from the crowd?

3. Have you messed up this phase in the past? Have you pitched a business idea too soon, asked for advice too soon, or been a taker? When you look back, can you see the mistake you made?

4. How can you ask someone about the current value they're seeking? I've already shared a few ways with you. "What projects are you working on right now? Is there anything I can do to help you grow your business? What's a person like you doing in a place like this?" Think of a

couple of your own, or convert these into your own way of speaking.

Activity

There are two levels to this activity. One is hard and will push you outside your comfort zone, but it will give you a great value. If you decide that it's too hard for you, we have a softer version.

COMPLIMENT TO DEATH: Hard Version

In this exercise, your goal is to compliment someone so much that they tell you to go away. I've tried this activity before and taken the conversation to the limit, and I've never successfully killed a conversation with compliments.

I was once talking to a couple, and I said, "You guys have to have a child. It's our only hope. Not only will your child be unbelievably beautiful, but they will be the leader of the resistance when the machines rise up against us. If you guys don't combine your amazing DNA, it could mean the end of the human race." Even after saying that the conversation continued.

I want you to see what it feels like to take your compliments to the limit, and I want you to be creative with it. You could compliment people on their strengths, but our goal is to be dynamic, not to be boring and obvious. If you walk up to a beautiful person and tell them how beautiful they are, the conversation will not go very well. But that's not we're trying to do here.

We want to use different compliments and see what happens. Complimenting their strengths is a landmine. Don't break a previous rule for this activity.

Just like we don't want to compliment their strengths, we don't want to be passive-aggressive. If you try and give a compliment that's a hidden insult, that's not a compliment, and it doesn't count.

The purpose of this activity is for you to feel what it's like to give pure value. Your goal is to focus only on the compliments you give. Even when your compliments are a little crazy, you'll still make people feel good.

No one wants the compliments to stop, so they will stay in alignment with the value you give them. I want you to feel what it's like and how people react when you give them pure value.

Seek Value: Easy Version

If the first exercise is too hard or pushes you beyond what you can do, that's okay. The goal of these exercises is just to give value. Here is a simpler activity that can achieve the same goal.

You're going to have ten conversations in which you're only allowed to focus on two topics: seeking value and giving value. Value-seeking is asking people questions with the purpose of finding out what's important to them right now.

When you're checking out at the grocery store, you can ask questions like, "What do you do when you're not working here? What's your family like? Are you working on some side projects? Are you going to night school?"

I want you to experiment to find the right way to ask value-seeking questions. The way you ask these questions will be different from the way I do.

Most people in my industry ask me about the projects I'm working on and how they can help. They completely focus on giving value. You can do this, as well. All you have to do is ask, "Is there anything I can do to help you in your business right now?"

When you know someone, that's an easy question to ask. If you don't know someone very well, it can be a little more difficult.

When you're at the checkout counter, you could ask, "Would it help you if I went to your manager and said you did an amazing job? You're awesome at your job and I want to help you out." You never know. It could help them a lot – you might even get them a raise.

Most of the time, when a customer approaches the manager they are trying to get someone fired. But if you tell the manager how great the cashier is doing, it could even save their job.

It's possible that something good will come your way when you do this activity, but I don't want you to expect that the manager will give you a coupon or something.

When we give value, amazing things can happen, but that's not why we do it. Please disconnect from expectations. Giving value can get you amazing things, but those are just nice side effects. Your ultimate goal is to make each person you talk to feel better about themselves.

Go out and experiment. Make ten people feel better about their lives. It can be people at an event, in the social settings where you've been practicing, or people you encounter in your daily life. When you've done that, you can join me in the next chapter.

[8] Hint: my favorite drink is a White Russian.

[9] I'm not in this category, and I *love* when people shoot video reviews and testimonials for me!

8

FAVORS ARE MUSCLE

In this important chapter, we are going to dig deep into the mechanism behind favors.

When I was younger, I had this belief that favors were a type of currency. If someone did a favor for you, you would owe them something. My life was defined by a series of obligations and expectations.

I would keep track of the people I owed a favor to and the people who owed me a favor. I would build up goodwill with certain people to the point where I'd done enough small favors for them that I thought I had earned one big favor. I became like Scrooge from *A Christmas Carol*, counting my favors in an 1800 ledger on a cold winter night.

When people realize that you see them as a number on a ledger, it dramatically increases how much they dislike you. People don't like to be measured that way, and you burn relationships due to misinterpretation.

If you do a favor for someone, you might feel like it's a number three on a scale of ten, while they feel like it's a number two. When they return the favor, they'll do a number-two favor, and you'll feel like the ledger is not even, but they'll feel like it is.

This happens all the time because it's impossible to put a numerical, trackable value on two different favors.

Is giving me a ride to school in the morning the same thing as me picking you up late at night when your car runs out of gas? How can you compare the equality of those two things? When you start analyzing, you'll say, "You were already on your way to school, so it's a smaller favor. I had to go out of my way to pick you up at the gas station, so it's a big favor."

Many people spend their entire lives counting and tracking favors. This mindset will trap you. You'll spend all your time trying to measure something that is immeasurable, and, in the end, you'll end up feeling disappointed with the level of favors people do for you.

Even worse is when someone forgets that you did them a favor. You may do something nice for someone, like getting them a job interview or introducing them to a friend, which may end up in an amazing result, like getting a great job or getting married. Those are level ten favors, and they may just forget that you made it happen.

People forget all the time, and it's not malicious. We just have a lot of things going on.

I forget projects I'm working on or people I'm talking to all the time. If I miss an email from you, it's possible that the conversation could die if you don't send a follow-up.

But it's not malicious.

Between checking emails, coaching clients, working on ghostwriting projects, running my businesses, and spending time with my family, a few emails slip through the cracks.

If that happens, you could feel like I'm ignoring you, and you could get offended. We go from missing a message because I have too much going on to someone getting offended. The problem escalates because we have this favor mindset.

Even more powerful is when someone helps me on a project and then asks me to record a video saying how great their work was. There are frequent times when I can't hop in front of a camera right away, so, despite my best intentions, it doesn't happen. By the time I'm outside with my camera on a day without rain, I have forgotten the request of a few days earlier. Not because it's not important, but because I'm working on many projects, and my kids keep me up all night.

A few years ago, a friend of mine was about to break up with her boyfriend, and I talked her out of it. They are still together because I was there in that one pivotal moment.

Does this mean she owes me a marriage-level favor? I'm pretty sure she doesn't even remember anymore.

The idea that favors are zero-sum with a fixed value or that you could run out of favors is a poisonous mindset that we want to get rid of.

Unlimited Favors

A favor is just another way of giving value. You're just doing something nice for someone.

When you are transitioning to this mindset, you will have to learn calibration. When you go from never doing favors for anyone to doing giant favors all the time, the people around you won't know how to adapt. You want to calibrate the level of the favors you do to fit you and your environment.

When we look at favors, we sometimes think that they depend upon the connection we have with someone. When you reach a certain level of connection, you think you can ask for one favor from them, and you don't want to waste it. It becomes like this golden favor in a genie's lamp.

Favors and relationships don't work that way. Favors are a muscle. When you do more favors, you become stronger and more effective at giving value.

Just like when you're strengthening the muscles in your body, you don't have to do giant, exhausting favors to strengthen your favor muscles.

Some of the most successful people I know are defined by their Rolodex. These are the people you know that you can reach out to. Often, you can do something as simple as introducing person A to person B and giving them a new connection. They gain a new relationship thanks to you, and you have barely put in any effort.

When you transition from the mindset of counting favors to simply doing as many as you can, it removes a lot of stress from within your heart.

This is the first and most amazing benefit of thinking of favors as a muscle - all the stress and negative emotions that come with balancing the favor ledger disappear. You no longer invest any energy in tracking your favor ledger, and that saved energy can go into doing favors for other people.

I don't track who owes me favors anymore. It may take me months or even a year to notice if someone never reciprocates the favors I do for them. When I notice, I simply stop doing favors for that one person, and there's no emotional pain that comes with it.

Think of favors as a universal thing. Don't assign a favor to each person. Instead, think of it as how many total favors you put out into the world.

On Shark Tank, Kevin O'Leary once said, "Here's how I think of my money: As soldiers. I send them out to war every day. I want them to take prisoners and come home, so there are more of them." That's exactly how I see favors.

Favors are little soldiers you put out into the world. The more you put out there, the more likely you are to capture more favors that will come back your way.

Favors are a way of investing without spending money, and they can massively leverage your income. As much as my business is built around writing books and selling products, the majority of my revenue is generated from favors.

The favors I put out into the world bring people to me with the same mindset. My business wouldn't be where it is right now without the favor soldiers that I have sent out into the world.

The second benefit is that you don't kill things off too soon. When you're tracking favors, they often come with a clock. There's a certain time expectation to return favors.

If you do a favor for me, your favor clock might be three months. If my favor clock is six months, there's a problem. Four months after you do a favor for me, you'll be annoyed that I haven't returned the favor, but I'll think I still have two whole months before it's a problem. At five months, it's too late, and you'll cut me off.

I've seen this before where people kill the relationship because the person didn't return a favor fast enough.

Some of the best return favors happen at around the three-year mark.

I have a friend who became a millionaire in his twenties and is now a full-time angel investor. He became massively successful and unbelievably wealthy because of a couple of favors that brought back their prisoners after three years in the field.[10]

Here's what happens. You do a small favor for someone, and the opportunity for them to return that favor doesn't come up. Then, three years later, a massive favor comes up, and your small favor is returned for a giant favor.

When you put favors out into the world, their value increases over time. When you get that three-year favor, the person you did a $100 favor for could send $10,000 your way.

When you're not worried about the timeline, the favor has the time it needs to mature, grow, and flower to deliver that beautiful fruit.

The third benefit is that you're rich. You have an infinite resource that you can convert into money.

We often undervalue our most valuable skills, assets, and resources. When you are good at something that other people can't do, it's a valuable resource that you can share in the form of favors.

Unfortunately, most people let their boss determine the value of your skill. Your boss will pay you the absolute lowest possible amount to get you to perform your job. Every dollar they don't pay you ends up in their pocket. This doesn't not mean they are paying what a job is actually worth. A plumber working for a large company might get paid $50 an hour, but, if the same plumber went out on his own, he could charge $200 an hour.

It's not market value that determines what a favor is worth – a favor is worth whatever the person you do it for feels that it is worth.

A plumber is a genius in the bathroom. He understands something that I don't. But people would usually place a plumber lower on the ladder than a millionaire. If you look at a plumber and a millionaire as two experts in different fields, they have parity.

It's useful for someone to have an expert in every different area within their Rolodex. No matter how rich you are, it's worthwhile to be friends with a plumber that you trust so that you can have someone who could advise you when you have a plumbing problem. It's not about getting free work. It's about making sure you don't make a mistake.

Wisdom is valuable. Someone can ask you questions, and, in return for your knowledge, an hour of your time could be worth $500 or even $10,000, depending on the field of expertise. Dealing with problems is about more than the cost. It's about the stress, frustration, and time spent helping someone else.

I used to be friends with a hairstylist who was amazing at what he did but never leveraged his skills. I always tried to bring him into my circle of wealthy friends, but he didn't perceive his expertise as equivalent to all the other people in our circle who had gone to college and had fancy degrees.

We have this perception in our society that rich people look down on poor people. More often than not, the disparity in a relationship comes from the poorer person. Just like when someone acts like a fan, they lock themselves into that lower position.

Believe in yourself and the value of your expertise.

This book directly ties into all of my other main teachings. You must understand your own value and the value of the things you do.

We've talked about looking for areas where you have strength. You can use those areas of strength and knowledge to give away favors.

You never know which favor someone is going to remember and which favor is going to turn massive dividends. The ability to throw out favors all the time is freeing.

You have an unlimited currency that you can use to your advantage.

Favors in Context

Doing favors is a powerful tool, but the possibility of a favor is just as powerful.

If you meet someone who is looking for schools for their children, you could say, "I know the principal at this school. Send me a message tomorrow, and I'll introduce you."

This hooks into what we were talking about earlier. When someone is seeking a specific value, you don't have to do the favor instantly. You can use it to guarantee a follow-up communication and to motivate them to want to talk to you later.

We're planting a seed, and, in some situations, it makes sense to do so. You're not going to call a kindergarten principal in the middle of the night from a cocktail party. It would be weird to do the favor right then and there, but it's totally logical to do it in the middle of the day.

As you go through this process, you'll have to calibrate. You'll discover that men and women interpret favors differently.

We've all seen the man in the dating world who's trapped in the friend zone. He buys the girl extravagant gifts, thinking, "If I just buy this girl a car, she'll fall in love with me." When we look at it from the outside, we can see why that's crazy, but people caught in the moment can't see that, and they make this mistake.

If you do a favor that's too big too soon, it's open to misinterpretation. I've seen it happen most often in the dating world, but it could certainly happen in any context.

As you develop and hone your favor skills, you'll learn to

start with small favors and see how people respond before you move onto bigger favors.

The fourth benefit of the mindset that favors are muscle is that it is unbelievably magnetic.

Successful people believe that favors are muscle, while unsuccessful people don't. These two groups attract like-minded people and repel the others. If you treat favors like muscle, you will attract others who treat them the same way. If you track favors, you'll attract other trackers.

If you do three or four favors for someone who's tracking them, they'll become overwhelmed trying to figure out how to repay your four favors. Like a person dodging a bookie, they'll go radio silent and try to disappear.

I've had people disappear from my life because they felt like they owed me something that they'll never be able to repay, even though I never called them about the debt and don't even think of it as a debt.

It's not the successful person that's terminating the relationship; it's the junior person who feels like they can never give enough value back to achieve parity. Instead of stressing out about repaying favors, all they have to do is change their mindset.

When I started this principle, I was very close to broke, but, if you looked at my Rolodex, you would assume that I was a millionaire because all of my friends were millionaires. I was barely making rent on an East London apartment, and most of my friends were flying in private jets.

People are attracted to mindset, and changing your mindset is how you can accelerate your social and financial improvement. If you just keep putting favors into the world, more people with high value, quality, integrity, and honesty will be drawn to you. This principle will be a magnet for the type of people you want in your life.

At a work party, the CEO of the entire company could end up spending the entire evening with you because there is something magnetic about you. This principle is what will attract the people you want to like you.

Reflection Questions

1. Have you ever lost a friendship over a favor? Who ended the friendship, the person who did the favor or the person who received the favor?

2. In the past, did you look at favors as a finite resource? Has it limited you? Has it caused you anxiety? Did you spend time tracking your favors and how big they were?

3. Do you see how changing this mindset can free you from all that time, energy, and emotion?

4. Imagine your life six months from now when you've completely transitioned to this mindset. You spend your time pumping favors into the world and putting good Karma out there.

How will your life be different? What will your life be like? How will people perceive you? What will be the great aspects of your life?

This is a moment for you to imagine a better future so that it can become your goal as we work through this process.

Activity

This activity has two parts to help you master the mindset of favors as muscle.

The first part is to go to your experimentation environment and practice your calibration. As you talk to people, you're going to do continuously bigger favors until you get a negative reaction. Start small, and work your way up until you see where the barrier is.

As you experiment, I want you to get creative to find which level works best for you. You can introduce two people or buy someone a drink. Getting someone a job or buying drinks for the entire bar is a little too big.

Through my own experimentation, I have found how to calibrate my favors. I do favors differently for each environment. I have to calibrate my favors to fit gender, the nature of the relationship, and how long I've known the person.

Through experimentation, you'll find your own calibration. Everyone is different, and people will respond to you differently than how they would for someone else.

Maybe you will find that women respond better to your favors, or that you need to do smaller favors for men and bigger favors for women. Calibration is necessary to find out how they respond to you specifically.

The second part is to start planting seeds within your own social circle. You're going to start implementing small favors without expectation. Remember, the goal is to be without intent. Doing a favor without expecting a return is a great way to implement this mindset.

Start doing small favors that are within your power and that don't mean much to the people around you. The goal is to just see how they react to you doing favors, as well as seeing which opportunities you have to do favors.

Just plant small seeds to see what happens. These favors probably won't come back to you from that particular person. But, you'll see that, as you do something for one group, something cool will come back to you from another group.

Try these two exercises and see how your life changes. I guarantee you that people will start treating you a little differently.

[10] You can hear the entire story on the Serve No Master podcast episode two.

9
OPEN LOOPS

An open loop is a psychological phenomenon that states that people remember tasks better when they're uncompleted. For the sake of what we're learning in this book, an open loop is simply a story you've started to tell but don't finish right away.

It's a powerful and effective storytelling technique. You often see magicians use this tactic, and I have even used it multiple times in this book.

When I say, "I'm going to explain this in a later chapter," I am opening a loop. When I say, "Remember when I talked about this?" I am closing that loop. I use open loops in my books as a technique to encourage my readers to continue reading and close the loops.

There's this old radio show I used to listen to as a child called, "And That's the Rest of the Story." They would tell you this amazing story about a celebrity, but they wouldn't tell you who it was until the end of the show. They would open the loop by saying, "You have to wait until the end of the show to find out who we're talking about." They would close that loop by saying,

"And that man was Abraham Lincoln. And that's the rest of the story."

In conversations, we can use small loops that open and close within the course of a few minutes. A simple example is to say, "The craziest thing happened at work today. I'm going to go grab a drink and come back to tell you about it." This is a good way to encourage someone to wait for you to come back to have the conversation.

There are certain loops that are programmed into us, like answering the phone, and others that you have to manually open in a conversation. The stronger the loop, the stronger the desire the person has to close it.

If you read a lot or watch a lot of movies, open loops are called foreshadowing. It's the simple idea of planting a hint about the future.

When you're in a conversation, it's useful to start conversational threads that you don't finish immediately. You can open a loop at the very beginning of a conversation, and you can close it whenever you want to.

At the beginning of this book, I mentioned a conversational starter. "I love your outfit. My sister told me to say something when I see good fashion in the world."

You might not have noticed it, but there is a small open loop in this statement. I never said who my sister is. Did you wonder who she designs for? Did you think you might recognize her brand name? Opening a loop is planting a seed that the other person wants to see flourish.

In the previous chapter, I mentioned that you can tell someone you'll give them value at a later time. "I know this amazing doctor. Message me tomorrow and I'll send you his contact details." This is also an open loop. There is a reward waiting for them in the future if they maintain the relationship with you.

This is the way a lot of friendships start. Before you think that this is too mercenary, imagine what would it be like if you were on the receiving end. If I decided that I wanted to be friends with you and launched a campaign of awesome things to make your life better, would you be upset? Of course not. There's no better way to make someone like you than to make their life awesome.

Learning to control the loop is about learning to control yourself. As much as the other person wants the loop to be closed, so do you. When you first try this technique, you'll want to finish the loop immediately.

Loops are a bit like Christmas. We all love Christmas Eve more than Christmas Day because we love that anticipation.

With a bit of practice, you'll learn how to hold off on closing the loop to give the other person a chance to enjoy the wait. People love anticipation. If you can learn to use that to your advantage, you'll be unstoppable.

I'm working on my first big fiction book right now, and a key element is the hero's journey. The perfect prototype for the hero's journey is the movie *Star Wars*.

In *Star Wars*, you watch a hero, Luke, fail a few times before he manages to defeat the villain, Darth Vader. If he confronted the villain and won within the first five minutes, no one would enjoy that movie.

People enjoy going through a period of mild suffering before they find success. It gives us more satisfaction to know that we struggled for it.

When you open a loop, take your time to close it. It will increase the satisfaction of your conversation partner.

The easiest way to practice this is to use your best stories that we worked on earlier. Take a few of these stories and stack them. Start five stories in a row but don't close any of the loops.

"I was at the mall yesterday, and the weirdest thing happened when I was trying to get a haircut. Actually, that reminds me of two weeks ago when I went to the bank and saw someone with a clown mask. Speaking of clowns…"

Do you see what happened there? You can start several stories at a time, and, as long as there is a connection between them, it doesn't sound weird or intentional. You only need to close the last story at the end, and the rest act as little seeds that encourage the person to continue talking to you.

Aren't you curious about the haircut story, or the bank story? These are the previews that will encourage people to stick around for the end of the movie.

You can use an open loop to create a bridge between the initial conversation and a future event. If you make the event sound amazing and provide benefits for your event, they will be more inclined to go.

Instead of saying, "Do you want to go out to dinner with me and listen to two hours of my stories?" you could give them a real incentive to go out with you. "I'm going to a White Wedding, and I'd love for you to come with me. Everyone dresses up like it's a bad 80s wedding movie, and they have a DJ who only plays 80s music. It's an unbelievably good time, and everybody there will love you."

White Weddings are one of my favorite events in London. It's so fun to dress up in terrible 80s clothes, and it's still a great way to have a good experience with someone.

Do you see how we're opening a loop here? We're providing future benefits for someone to show up.

Even though some people call it bridging, this is still an

open loop. You're opening something and providing incentives for people to show up and see the end of that loop.

When you plant the seeds of all the areas in which you are strong, people want to hear more about it. When I tell people that I'm a ghostwriter, they want to hear more. They can see that there are things about me that they don't know yet, and that keeps the relationship interesting.

If you knew everything about me, you wouldn't be interested. If I gave you a Jonathan Manual filled with my strengths, weaknesses, skills, and every other little detail about me, you would only contact me if there was something on the sheet you wanted right now.

If I gave you the same sheet, but half it was redacted, you would have to talk to me to fill in the blanks. This is your motivation to have a second conversation. You don't know everything about me, so you can't make a decision yet. Instead, you have to continue to get to know me little by little.

I don't want people to decide if they like me or not based on one conversation. I want to have three or four different conversations in different locations. The more time you get in different locations, the more memories people create of you.[11]

For most people, memories are based on backgrounds. You could work in an office sitting next to the same person for years. But, when you leave that job, you will barely remember them because they're stored in a single file in your memory.

The person you dated for two weeks and went on ten crazy dates with is a much stronger memory, not only because it's an emotional memory, but also because you have more locations in your memory with that person.

If you only went to see movies with that person, you

might not remember them very well because they only have the movies as their location in your memory.

It's not just the level of emotional engagement you have to a person that keeps them in your memory, but it's also the variety of backgrounds.

Opening loops is a way to give yourself more chances. Small loops give you more time within a single conversation. If you have three minutes to impress someone, you can gain five extra minutes by opening a bunch of loops. That person will gladly give you more time just to see how they close.

If you open bigger loops, you can turn a two-minute introduction into a one-hour conversation that can lead to follow-up communications. This is how I form all of my business relationships.

Whether you call it bridging, planting seeds, or opening loops, it's all the same idea of planting value now and harvesting it later.

Reflection Questions

1. When you hear a ringing phone, how strong is your desire to answer it? The next time you hear a ringing phone, try to resist it and see what it feels like.

2. Think about some open loops that you've experienced. Maybe someone was singing the lyrics to a song but didn't finish it, or maybe they were singing them wrong. How did you feel? Were you frustrated? Did you feel the need to shout out the right answer or finish the lyrics for them? That's a perfect example of an open loop. Write down the times you've experienced this.

3. Think about some loops that you can open in your ideal conversation. What are some topics you can start without finishing? Try to find topics that would stack well together. Remember, stacking is when you open three or four topics or observations and only close one. Make sure you can transition from one topic to the next without appearing intentional.

4. How can you turn your areas of strength, expertise, and knowledge into loops you can open? Opening loops about your strengths get you a chance at a second conversation so you can turn conversations into phone numbers.

Open Loop Activity

We're going to be a little bit devious to see how powerful open loops are.

Go back to your practice environment, open a loop, and then leave the conversation. Start telling a story, then say, "Excuse me, I'm going to grab a drink." Go across the room and don't come back. Don't go home, but don't go back to the person.

If you open a loop correctly, the person will find you and demand to hear the end of the story. It won't happen every time, but you'll see that it really does affect people. People have an urge to close loops. They want to hear the end of a story.

Use stories from previous activities and continue refining them with this activity. Take a few of your best stories, and just cut them into two pieces. Then, see if people try to get you to finish them and put them back into one piece.

If people don't want to hear the end of a particular story, it might not be a very strong story. That's okay. We're just testing the waters with this activity.

Your second activity is to observe. If you pay attention, you'll start to notice open loops everywhere, especially online. People use them when they want to make something go viral.

Go to a clickbait website to see how they phrase their headlines. It's always something along the lines of, "This astronaut came home on his son's birthday, and you'll never believe what happened next."

You'll have no problem finding these websites because they'll have the most clicks and likes, and they'll be trending on social media.

Write in your Journal some good headlines that you could repurpose and use for your own stories. Create two columns in your Journal. On the left-hand column, write out the headlines exactly as they appear. On the right-hand column, rewrite them in ways that you can use in conversations.

Take the clickbait structure and tailor it to fit you and your personality. These are great examples of open loops that you can use, and they can give you some ideas for how you can open your own loops.

[11] This is a continuation of the loop opened in the chapter on transitioning.

10

OPEN THE LINES OF COMMUNICATION

You now have the tools and the mindset to have good, short conversations. You can meet a stranger and have an enjoyable ten-minute conversation. When you go to business events with people you don't know, you can use the tools I've given you to be more successful.

However, that is not why you grabbed this book. You want to go further than just one interaction. Whether it's business relationships, friendships, or romantic partners, you want relationships that stick so that you can enjoy the fruits of your labor.

We've already discussed the power of opening loops so that someone wants to talk to you again. Now, we want to go beyond that and expand the breadth of communication to make you reachable.

Everyone has different ways of communicating. Their age, gender, and personality all play a role in their approach to communication. I've met people who only communicate via Twitter or Facebook Messenger. This is how they handle all their conversations from business to friendships. Some people prefer texting, and others prefer to talk on the phone.

When I form a business contact, I initially connect with them on Skype. I live internationally, so texting back and forth doesn't work for me. I find Skype superior to email because it offers real-time communication.

For my family members, I use WhatsApp and iMessenger. These two apps allow me to text them no matter where I am in the world. I can send videos and pictures of my children to family members without posting them on social media platforms for the whole world to see.

If you follow me on social media, you know how rarely I post anything about my children. I want them to decide when they're older how much of their lives to make public. Instead of posting pictures of them on social media, I only send them through private messaging to my family.

Everyone uses different communication tools, and some people have a level of priority for each tool that they use. When you meet someone, you want to know which lines of communication they use, and you want to get access to the best one.

When you first meet someone, it's hard to know whether their phone number or email address is more valuable. However, their personal email address is always more valuable than their business email address.

I have a dozen email addresses, and I can list them from the most public to the most private. I check my business emails once a day, but I check my personal email every time I get a new message. My personal email is usually only for important information that doesn't need a reply, so I make sure to always keep it open and updated.

If you get access to that highest-level email, it's almost like communicating with me in real time. Whereas I only check my business email once a day, I will see a personal email every few hours.

Rather than trying to guess the best way to communicate with each person you meet, we're going to take the breadth approach to form multiple connections. This will allow us to have a presence in someone's life.

People communicate differently depending on the platform they use. If you wanted to have a strong connection with me, you'd connect with me on Facebook, Skype, and email. Once you have created three lines of communication, the secret to creating presence is to have three distinct conversations.

I'm currently part of a four-way group chat that I should never have been invited to. Two people are trying to get me to ghostwrite for their client. In this group chat, they are discussing with the client how much he should pay me, and he will not respond.

Because it's in a group chat, I can see them chasing this totally non-responsive person, and it's continually lowering my expectations. They should have started a new chat without me because now I will be shocked if this project ever happens. This is what can happen when you use different chat mediums.

When you have multiple lines of communication with someone, you should have separate conversations on each of them. On Facebook, we could talk about my kids. On Skype, we could talk about my travel plans for my next event. Through email, we could discuss project ideas that we could collaborate on.

Having three distinct conversations strengthens our connection. Instead of forming one memory, we're forming multiple memories. As I hop between those threads, they get saved in different ways, and you take up more space in my memory.

There are two ways of branding yourself. The first way is to have the same picture of yourself on all of your social media platforms. If people constantly see that image, it strengthens the idea someone has of who you are.

The second method is to have a different image on each of your platforms. This helps someone paint a three-dimensional memory of you. Both ways are effective.

Avoid drawings and pictures of your dog or kids. If you're using a profile picture of something other than you, you're not forming a strong memory because the person won't think of you as real.

They will see that picture of a dog or a cartoon, and they won't really feel like they're talking to you. They'll subconsciously think they're talking to that dog or cartoon, and they're not forming memories of you.

When you first meet someone, it can be very unnatural to ask for multiple lines of communication. Instead of saying, "Can I have your phone number, your Skype, your Twitter, and your Facebook?" we should spread it out.

This process will take some experimentation to find the right calibration for you, but there are a few approaches to get multiple lines of communication.

The first is to ask at different points in the conversation. Early on, you could ask for their LinkedIn page. This will get you a business connection. Most people on this platform will connect with almost anyone because having a ton of connections strengthens your profile.

Once you're LinkedIn friends, later in the conversation, you could say, "I do most of my business via text." Then, you could swap numbers. Now, you have two different lines of communication.

Toward the end of the conversation, you could mention

a social group where you're strong. "I'm part of this group of artists, and we have a Facebook group. What's your Facebook? I'll invite you."

If you attach value or an open loop to each connection you ask for, it grounds what you're saying. Grounding is when you justify or give a reason for asking.

Grounding is a simple way to make you feel more comfortable asking for these connections. The more you practice and the more comfortable you become, you won't need to ground as much, but it is a good way to train to attach a benefit to every request.

Instead of saying, "I want your phone number so I can talk to you more," you could say, "I want your phone number so I can introduce you to that contact we talked about."

Simple things can be of huge value. An honest mechanic, a good painter, or a great pediatrician are valuable people you might have in your Rolodex.

If you have children, you know how hard it is to find a good pediatrician. We finally found a great one after sifting through loads of terrible ones. To find her, we had to go through loads of recommendations from friends and doctors. Knowing a good pediatrician may seem like a simple thing, but it can be of huge value to someone else.

As we've already discussed, you can use this value as an open loop, which can help you get another connection with someone. "I don't have his number with me, but if you give me your phone number, I can text his contact information to you tomorrow."

You could also give instant value at that moment. "If you give me your number, I can text you his contact information right now." The next time that person gets a text from you, they'll see the value that you already gave them, and they'll be more inclined to reply to your message. When your name pops up on their phone, all they'll see is that value you already gave them.

Giving value in the moment can be just as useful as opening a loop to give value later on. You just have to calibrate to figure out which one works best for you.

Each time you open a line of communication, your mindset should be to give value to justify this new connection.

Why You Need Multiple Connections

As you expand your lines of communication, more people are going to like you.

People plan their events in different ways. There's no universal way for how we handle our planning and how we communicate with others.

Some people plan all of their events by clicking the Yes button on Facebook events. If you look at their Facebook calendar, you can see everything they're going to do. If you were to look at my Facebook calendar, you would have no idea what I have going on.

The interesting thing about the "yes" button on these events is that of all the people who say they're going, many don't actually show up. It's not the best way to see what's happening, but it does give you a good sense of a person's calendar.

If the person you want to attract is the type to click Yes, you can follow the events they want to go to.

This gives you a two-fold advantage. First, you can run into these people, which gives you another location in their memory. Second, you can meet tons of other people just like them.

Other people do a lot of their planning via mass text. They'll send out a text to their social circle saying what they're doing this weekend, and they'll ask who wants to go.

There are a lot of younger people who make a living as promoters. They have a list of people who like certain events, and they let those people know when these events come up. A lot of this is done via text messaging, but there are plenty of promoters who post events on social media platforms.

The more lines of communication you have, the easier it is for you to connect with someone. You can meet up with them more often, and you can discover friends you have in common or hobbies you both share.

This is a two-way street. When you're seeing their profile, they're seeing yours. They're seeing connections you have in common, who you spend time with, and all the pictures that you post.

Just as you get to discover more about this person, they also get to background check you. Having multiple connections is mutually beneficial.

Having multiple lines of connections is great, but it's also dangerous. If they don't respond to your message on Facebook, it's tempting to message them on Twitter or text them. You should never open multiple lines of communication when you're not getting a reply on any of them. This puts you in the position of a jilted lover.

Mastering this type of communication takes practice, which is why we've been experimenting in low-risk environments. You're going to run into some hurdles, but having this experience helps you to overcome those hurdles.

As you continue to experiment, you'll find what works best for you. There is no definitive answer for how to communicate because everyone has their own way of using different communication tools.

There are a lot of different social media platforms because preferences change from person to person, from culture to culture. Some people like WhatsApp, some like Line, and others like Viber.

Technology changes so quickly that it would be pointless for me to tell you which one to use. By the time you read this, something new will be the best.

Instead of trying to find the single best line of communication, open as many lines as you can. Getting just two or three open lines will let you stay on their radar.

Sometimes people get behind on their replies. They have a thousand emails to reply to, so they might forget to reply to yours, or they might just be too overwhelmed to reply to you. Sometimes, it takes some thought and effort that people don't feel like investing to respond to emails.

However, when you message them on Skype, you can discuss the email there. This way, you won't be forgotten or pushed to the back burner.

Having multiple lines of communication increases your stickiness, your knowledge of each other, and the likelihood of staying in contact.

Reflection Questions

1. Take a look at how you communicate. Do you use multiple modes of communication? Do you prefer texting over Twitter or Skyping over phone calls? Look at each different mode of communication you use and rank them based on how you use them. Do you use them for business or for your personal life? Is this where you do your future planning?

2. Are there certain communication modes that you don't use? Maybe you don't have a Twitter account or a WhatsApp. Let's say one day you run into your dream husband, perfect business partner, or new best friend. If they only use an app that you don't have, how would you feel?

3. Do you see social media as a place of entertainment or a tool for improving your life and your business? Do you see them as a communication tool or something else? Write a full paragraph or two as you analyze how you use these tools.

4. Think about the people who you've lost touch with. Did you lose touch because you let an old email address fade away or one of you changed your phone numbers? Would you still be in contact with them if you had multiple lines of communication?

5. Do you see the value in opening multiple lines of communication? Do you see how it could ensure that you don't lose critical relationships?

Activity

Your first activity is to prune your social media. Each of your social media platforms is a tool, and you should have a clear idea of the purpose of each one.

You can have a Facebook profile filled with pictures that show off your frat-boy lifestyle. However, you cannot use this profile to attract a classy lady or try to land a high-end job.

If you try to be everything to everyone, you'll be nothing to nobody. Instead, each social media platform should have a specific purpose.

You can use LinkedIn to post your resume, your accomplishments, and your previous employment. If you own your own business, you can use it to generate more customers as part of a business funnel. If you use it correctly, people will want to hire you simply based on your profile.

For each of your social media profiles, you want to determine its purpose. Each of them should be used as a tool. If you're using it for simple entertainment, you're using it wrong, and you won't be able to connect with the people you want to.

If you want to keep using your Facebook as a place to display pictures of you and your friends getting wasted, that's fine. But, you should know that you can never share that Facebook account with anyone from a higher level. The last thing you want to do is give them evidence that you're from a lower level.

Go through each of your social media profiles and consider what each picture and post say about you. There is a price to pay when posting personal pictures and information. They are there forever for all the world to see.

If your Facebook is filled with posts about your ex, potential romantic partners are going to think you're needy, desperate, and not at all someone they want to date.

I've agonized after a break up just like everyone else. But, there is a price to pay when you put something on social media. It's there forever, and anyone can see it.

If you create a post about tricking your boss so you can

take the day off, your boss might find out and fire you, and people will see that you're not trustworthy. People will see that you're dishonest and proud of it.

It's worth it to prune your history. Make sure that your social media profiles are something you can be proud to show to other people.

Your second activity is to join all the different social media platforms and apps that are popular in your region. Line, WhatsApp, Viber, and Twitter are a few popular ones that you can start with.

Sign up for all of these, even if you don't use them. I have plenty of apps that I only use to communicate with one or two people, and some of them I haven't even used for a few years. It's good to have them just in case you meet someone who uses that platform.

When I first visited Thailand, I made the mistake of asking people for their phone numbers. In this country, asking for a phone number is considered weird.

Everyone there uses Line. I thought they were just saying "line" as in a telephone line. Actually, Line is the name of an app. I ended up with egg on my face because I didn't do the research. Now I use Line for everyone I meet in Thailand.

Do your research to find out which platforms are the most popular in your area and within the age group of the people you want to know. Then, join them. If you aren't quite sure, just join a bunch on your phone. It's always better to have too many platforms than to not have one when it comes up.

These two first activities are prep work. Once you have practiced implementing the techniques I've given you, you're ready for the third activity.

You're going to practice opening multiple lines of

communication and getting contact details on different platforms. The more you experiment and practice, the easier it will be. If you have practiced this with a hundred different people, you'll be ready when that perfect person comes along.

11

THE GOLDEN RULE

We all know this principle: Treat people the way you want to be treated. Even though everyone knows it, we all have to be reminded of it from time to time.

In our culture, we love to rank people. We rank them from one to ten based on beauty, money, height, career, or a whole slew of other factors. This is called thin slicing.[12] It's how we sort the world and the data we collect, and there's nothing wrong with doing it.

What is wrong is how we use that data. Many people treat those they consider beneath them like trash. They say they'll treat people better once they get to the top, but they already treat the people beneath them poorly. This is mindset is keeping you from getting to a higher level.

Many people at higher levels observe how you treat waiters to get a sense of how you treat people that are beneath you. If they see you treating them in a repulsive way, they will limit your relationship.

When you treat a poor person bad and a rich person well, the only difference between them is that one has money and the other doesn't. If that rich person loses their money, you would be just as mean to them as you were to the waiter. Why would they want to be friends with someone like that?

Truly successful people treat everyone well, and similar traits are magnetic. Bad people attract bad, and good people attract good.

If you enjoy being mean to waiters, you're probably friends with someone who enjoys that, too, and the two of you can be awful to the waiter together. Two people who are nice to waiters will fight over who should give the bigger tip. You can either make the world a better place or a worse place.

If I went out with you, and you spent the entire dinner being mean to the waiter, I wouldn't enjoy myself at all because I would spend the entire time apologizing for you.

Decide who you want to attract. Do you want to attract those who treat lesser people badly or those who treat lesser people well?

Remember, we're trying to climb social ladders. Most of the people that I meet and do business with are higher than me. If they treated lower people badly, there's no way I would be where I am today.

When I was still in the dating world, I would stand behind a woman and watch how she reacted to another guy approaching her. There was always the risk that she would fall in love with some other guy, but I really wanted to see how she treated strangers. If she was mean to him or said something terrible after he walked away, I knew I never wanted to meet her, because the real her was not the kind of person I wanted in my life.

I like situational starters so much because I can see how people treat strangers. I love waiting in long lines because it gives me a chance to have a great conversation with someone. When I'm in line behind someone I think I might want to talk to, I ask them, "Are you in line?" This is more of a test than a conversational starter.

Ninety percent of the people will turn around and start a conversation. Nine percent will say yes and turn back around. One percent will be incredibly rude. When someone is rude, it's a gift. You can save yourself so much time and effort because you find out within the first three seconds that this is not a person you want to talk to again.

This is why successful people watch how you treat strangers. Rather than just judging you based on how you look, they're judging you based on your behavior.

No matter where you are or what you're doing, someone will always be watching. Successful people watch your interactions. They are constantly collecting data to see who's the most important person. If you walk around the room and talk to every single person in a nice way, your perceived value can skyrocket.

Here's a trick to change how people see you. If you go to a bar filled with beautiful women, talk to all of them. Even if they completely shun you, you can use perception to create a win. You could walk away with your tail between your legs, or you could walk away with a smile on your face like she just said something flirtatious.

I have done this plenty of times. I have had conversations where the woman told me I was too ugly to even talk to. I'm not a very good-looking man, so people prejudge me all the time. Every time I get a bad reaction, I walk away with a smile as if it were a good reaction.

When you go around the room, talk to twenty people and act like each conversation went well, the most beautiful woman in the room will walk up to you and want to talk to you. She will think that every girl in the bar is talking to you, so she will want to know what she's missing.

You can use this tactic in plenty of other situations. The point is that you can alter perception by the way you react to things.

It's always better to respond positively to a bad experience.

Later, we're going to talk about the principle of dominating a venue or becoming friends with all the staff. If you just use the simple tools we've discussed, you can have a simple conversation with everyone.

This is where these two principles converge. Treating everyone well means that when you walk around the room talking to each of those people, you don't have to fake it. It's easier to be nice to everyone. You can walk around the room knowing all the staff, and your value goes up naturally.

Man of Strategies

I have a friend who's a street magician. He stands in front of you in a T-shirt and shorts, and a full-sized watermelon appears under his shirt. I have no idea how he does it, but he makes it appear every time.

When he goes to bars, he always gets mistaken for the owner, and he does this on purpose. Instead of looking at the conversation, he looks at how people perceive his conversations. He takes a meta approach to control the battlefield.

When he goes to a bar, he dresses very nicely. He doesn't look like a member of the staff, but he walks around clearing up dirty glasses from tables, which is what an owner generally does. He grabs finished glasses from tables and puts them on the bar to make it easier for the staff. He does this because he likes to be helpful.

He also likes to be in a place that looks nice. He doesn't like when glasses are scattered around because they can easily fall. When they shatter, this can affect the mood of the whole room and ruin a moment.

Let's say you're right about to exchange phone numbers with someone. When the glass shatters, you get distracted and the moment is gone. You don't end up exchanging phone numbers, and you never end up being friends with that person.

The third reason that he picks up those glasses is Meta. He only tells this reason to people who are very close to him. This is where he controls his environment and changes how people perceive him.

When people see someone well-dressed picking up glasses, they think he's the owner, and everyone wants to talk to the owner.

If you would ask him why he's cleaning up, he'll always tell you the first two answers. He won't lie and say he's the owner. He'll just tell you that he's cleaning up to make things easier for the employees and because he likes to be in clean bars.

As he's cleaning up, he also walks around and asks people if they're having a good time. He wants to make sure everyone is enjoying themselves, but this also helps to make people think he's the owner.

He likes to be in a strong social environment, and he knows just what to do to create the environment he wants. He is changing how every person in the room feels. He increases the mood of the room while minimizing the odds of a state break, which is an event that breaks the mood.

He is also altering his perceived value based on people's assumptions. Even when people find out that he is not the owner, they will still perceive him the same way because his answer is good, true, and elevates his social standing. They love that he is making sure they have a good time even though he's not being paid.

If you're dressed like an owner, people will like you. But if you're dressed like the staff, this will backfire. I made this mistake once, and I had to change my shirt because everyone was asking me for directions to the bathroom.

When employees find out what my friend is doing, they really appreciate it. It's nice for them, especially in an environment in which no one does this.

As you enter an environment, think about how you can give small amounts of value to the entire room. It's okay if that value also benefits you.

My friend benefits from cleaning glasses because people want to meet him, but he's still doing something nice for everyone there. He cleans up for the employees, and he's making the place nicer for the customers. It's a win for everyone.

When you do something that's a win for everyone, it's not a manipulative tactic. It's simply doing something mutually beneficial for everyone involved. It's okay to give people a good time so that they like you. That's all that friendship is.

Reflection Questions

1. Have you ever seen someone treat an employee like garbage? How did it make you feel when you saw that?

2. Do you want to be in a relationship with someone who treats lesser people badly? What will you do when they decided to treat you badly?

3. Do you treat people the way they should be treated, or do you ignore them because you're just trying to get through your day?

4. Have you ever observed the way someone treated someone else? When it was poor treatment, did it change your perception of that person? Did you decide not to be friends with or do business with them?

5. Write down five to ten people in your life that you haven't been treating as well as you should. It could be a waiter, the person who takes your ticket at the movies, a cashier, or someone else.

Activity

This is going to be a light activity because we've already done something very similar in previous chapters. I want you to go out and talk to strangers with the sole purpose of making their day a little better. Your goal is to be more conscious of the people who are outside your target.

If you're going to a meetup at a restaurant, talk to every staff member. Find out their names and give them a compliment or piece of value. If you get to know all the staff, you'll be well-known to them at future events. Instead of just being one of the group of people they're serving, you'll be special to them.

The more you experiment with this activity, the more you'll notice that your value will go up with the people in and around your group.

[12] Thin slicing is covered in great detail in the book *Blink* by Malcolm Gladwell.

12

UNLOCK YOUR SUPERPOWER – GOOD VIBES ARE THE ULTIMATE VALUE

If you've been paying attention and working on the exercises in this book, this chapter won't come as a surprise. Fun is a superpower, and we're going to dig into the effectiveness of this principle.

In life, our level of control ebbs and flows. As children, we don't get to choose our school, what we eat, when we go to bed, or who we get to play with. As we get older, we have more control over our lives. We get to decide where we go to college, where we work, and who we spend our time with.

Wealth and freedom are defined by having choice. The higher your social and financial level, the more choice you have. When you have a lot of choices, you can choose who you spend time with, and you can invest in people that you like.

Most entrepreneurs choose their path so that they never have to work with someone they don't like ever again. Everywhere I've ever worked, there have been people that I didn't like or people that didn't like me. Sometimes they were jealous of my job, sometimes they thought I was too young or too old, and sometimes we had different work styles that just didn't mesh well.

It doesn't matter where you work or what your work style is. There's always going to be someone who you just don't click with. We don't often get to choose our jobs based on our friendships. We generally choose our jobs so we can make money.

The people we want to connect with who are higher up socially, economically, and relationally have more choice, and, if they have the choice, they will always choose to spend time with those they like over those they don't like.

The point of this book is to learn to be more likable, and people like to be around those who make them feel good. More specifically, people want to be around people who help them have fun.

Everyone has a different definition of fun. The way I defined fun in college is different from the way I would define fun now that I'm twice as old.

As we build our conversational skills and dial into the type of people we want to attract, we can figure out how they define fun.

You may remember some questions that I asked you earlier in this book. "If you never had to work again, what would you spend your time doing? What's your favorite thing about yourself? What do you love doing?"

These are all questions designed to find out how people define fun. As you become someone who focuses on ensuring people have fun, you become everyone's favorite person.

I also mentioned earlier my friend who walks around at bars and restaurants picking up empty glasses and asking people if they're having a good time. His priority is that everyone is having fun, and this is his way of showing others where his priorities are.

He's not only changing how people perceive him, but he's also ensuring that people are experiencing their highest order value.

It doesn't matter how rich, beautiful, or intelligent people are. We are all driven by the desire to have a good time. Sometimes it can go down the path to hedonism, and sometimes people become daredevils searching for the next crazy thrill. But, at their core, people are driven by fun, and, if you can provide fun, people will automatically like you more.

You could be the poorest person at a party full of billionaires, but, if you're making sure everyone is having fun, you'll have a higher value than anyone else in the room.

Bringing people fun is equal to any other value, whether it's beauty, intelligence, strength, or political power. These are all wonderful attributes to have, but, at the end of the day, people are driven by fun.

How many politicians risk everything for fun, usually the dirty kind? Pretty much every politician abuses their power. They have the power to make the world a better place and make important changes, but the majority of them exchanges it for some good feelings and short-term fun.

People think power is the ultimate goal when, in reality, it's the penultimate goal. Power is just a stepping stone on the way to what you really want, which is the ability to have lots of fun.

Your mindset should be to look at every environment as a place where you can ensure everyone's having fun, and there are a few different ways you can generate fun for the people around you.

One of the ways that I'm well known for is throwing parties. When I host a party, I don't have any fun. I work so hard to ensure that everyone else is having fun that I am exhausted by the end of it. I'm like a reverse vampire. People suck the energy out of me while I ensure that they all have an amazing time.

I only do one party every year or two, and it generates enough friendships, relationships, goodwill, and business that my family's future is secure for the time being.

Fun is a critical currency. When I sacrifice one night a year to ensure that everyone is having an amazing time, it is worth it for the long-term payoff.

As you form new connections and have conversations, we want to bring in one more conversational thread. We already know how to find the value someone is seeking, what's important to them, and the areas where they're weak and strong, but now we want to look at how they define fun.

It's impossible to say objectively how to have fun because it's different for everyone. For some people, fun is a game of miniature golf. For others, it's going to the movies. A person's definition of fun can even change during different phases of their lives.

Instead of guessing how someone defines fun, we can just ask them. "What do you like to do for fun?" is one of my favorite questions because it helps me decide if they're someone I want to hang out with. If we have the same idea of fun, we can have a great time together without working too hard.

It's great if you both have the same definition of fun, but it's not always the case. Sometimes, having fun is more of a value exchange. If there's someone higher up than me who has a value I want, like promoting one of my products, I can exchange that value for having fun with them doing something they like. Even if I'm not enjoying what we're doing, there's a value exchange in the interaction. They get to have fun, and I get a promotion.

When you're interacting with people, add this final interrogative layer to discover how they define fun. It's a question we must ask because it can always change.

My current definition of fun has changed dramatically from what it was a few months ago.

This year was tough. Every member of my family except for me had a major medical incident and had to spend time in the hospital. That put an unbelievable amount of stress on my body, mind, and bank account.

Surgery for infants is not cheap, and it's hard to work when your child is in the hospital. I spent huge amounts of money while making less money, and it became the centerpiece of my universe.

Now that my children are in the healing period, we're still limited because they're not allowed to get in the water. I live on an island, we have an amazing pool, and the kids aren't allowed to get wet. That means that I don't get wet.

The things I used to love to do, I can't do right now. In a week, I may be allowed to, but for now it feels wrong to play in the water when my children can't.

My definition of fun has shifted. Even though I want to take my kids swimming, my sense of priorities has shifted because of this phase in my life. Three months from now, it will have shifted again, once my children are better.

As we go through times of challenge, our focuses shift. Guessing what someone does for fun is too hard because you have no way of knowing everything that is going on in their life. You can check out their Facebook page or see what they're saying on social media. Or, you could just start a conversation with them and ask.

Reflection Questions

1. Write down your ten favorite things to do for fun and rank them in order of highest to lowest priority. Keep in mind how much time they take and how much they cost.

Some of the things we love to do are difficult to do or cost too much. I love snowboarding, but it's impossible because I live in the tropics. I would have to travel internationally in order to snowboard.

You may have things on your list that you can't do quite yet, and we want to factor that in.

2. Throughout your life, your definition of fun has changed. Look back at your definitions from high school, college, after college, in your thirties, in your forties, and now. It depends on how old you are and where you are in life, but write down what you thought was fun at different stages in your life. We want to see how your definition of fun has changed.

3. Think about someone you know (or you have heard of) whose main value is to ensure that the people around them are having fun. There are plenty of famous bands who have a person traveling with them whose only job is to make sure everyone is having fun.

Activity

There are three parts to this activity. First, you're going to talk to all the people you know, including your friends, spouse, children, and colleagues, and ask them how they define fun. I recommend you write down their answers in your contact book, on your phone, or even in your Journal.

The more we know about how someone puts a smile on their face, the easier it is to be the one to put it there. As you go through your friends, you may have your guesses confirmed, or you may be surprised by their answers.

You may have been having fun with these people in the wrong way. Knowing how your friends define fun will help you redirect your relationships. You may have seen that classic television scene where the distant father brings his daughter a gift, and she says, "I would have loved this six years ago, Dad. You're so out of touch." By updating our definition of fun for each of our friends, we can avoid living out that scene.

Your second activity is inquisitive. Go out into the world and, for each person you interact with, focus on finding out their definition of fun.

There are plenty of different ways to ask people how they define fun, so it's your job to find the right phrasing that works for you. To help get you started, I'll give you a few questions you can ask.

What do you like to do for fun?

What's your hobby?

What do you like to do when you're not working?

If you never had to work again, what would you spend all your time doing if nobody would ever judge you and money wasn't an issue?

WE'RE GOING to go through a learning phase. We're honing in on how different people define fun, and we're starting to understand the similarities and differences between people.

You may discover that all the people you talk to are on

the same wavelength as you, and you all define fun as playing golf. You may discover that men your age have similar answers to each other, while women your age have their own similar answers. Once you know how people define fun, you can adjust your approach to how you communicate with people.

Your third exercise is to ensure that everyone you meet is having fun. From now on, we're going to add fun as a critical element to every piece of our process.

When you talk to people, do everything you can to make sure they're having fun. When you invite people to events and you open and close a loop, you should say something like, "You should come. You would have so much fun. Everyone would like you."

We want to make fun a seed we plant. If you tell someone to do something because they'll have fun, they're going to want to do it. This works whether you're inviting people to a speaking engagement, a party, or a date. No one would turn down a date if they were guaranteed to have a great time.

Once you understand the power of fun, you'll be that much closer to getting anyone to like you.

13

EASY WAYS TO GIVE VALUE

I'm going to give you a few more tools that you can use when you're giving value.

When you're first learning this process, it can be a little overwhelming to come up with ideas to give value to everyone. I'm going to share with you a few ways that work in specific situations. Hopefully, these can get your juices flowing so you can come up with even more ways.

A lot of my networking is built around business, which is why this book leans in that direction. As much as we want to make friends, I want to show you how to go to that next level. These techniques are geared toward business networking, but they apply to concerts and festivals for friendship networking, if that's what your goal is.

Designated Driver

You may have some experience with being the designated driver in college, and you may have been burned. People in college can be jerks.

When I was in college, people would always try to get

the designated driver to drink. I even knew some people who dubbed themselves, "The best designated drunk driver." I guess that means they felt they were good at driving drunk, and it's horrible to think about.

Once we leave college and become mature adults, our perspectives change. We start to respect driving, and having someone sober who will drive you to and from a party becomes valuable and respected.

Being the designated driver doesn't necessarily mean driving drunk people around. All you're doing is acting as the transportation for people you want to attract.

This technique works in almost any situation. If you go to an out-of-town conference, you have a massive opportunity. You could rent a nice town car for the weekend, and, because everyone else has traveled to be there, you know that you'll have a captive audience.

If you drive people to and from dinner or events, you'll have at least ten minutes with the people you want to like you. You do them a favor and give them value, and they'll be forced to talk to you in the car. It's a great opportunity to meet new people.

People could easily grab a taxi or an Uber, but I know from experience that it's so much easier when someone just has a car. You can avoid waiting in long taxi ranks, and you don't have to pay attention to the meter to make sure you're not getting ripped off. It cuts out so much stress by having someone you know drive you around.

When I was younger, if someone wanted to be my apprentice, I would have them drive me to meetings, dinner, and events. I had the convenience of having my own driver, and they got to spend time with me learning what I had to teach them.

In high school, you might remember that one person in

your group of friends who had a car. Or maybe you've seen the guy in a band who's only there because he has a van that can fit all their gear.

Transportation is incredibly valuable. When you translate it into relationships, you get more time on the clock, and people will remember that you were the person who drove them around. Even if it's just for a weekend, it's a great technique to make people remember and like you.

If there's a group of people you want to be friends with, all you have to do is offer to drive them to a festival or another event that they want to go to. It may limit your fun, but it increases the fun of everyone else.

When we're trying to expand our social circle, it sometimes becomes necessary to diminish our fun and increase other people's fun. You just have to remember that it's not a permanent situation, and it's incredibly valuable to get you where you want to be.

Buy a Round

Buying a round of drinks gets you an unbelievable amount of goodwill.

In English pubs, there's a weird culture of buying rounds. A group of sixteen friends would all take turns buying a round for everyone else. This does not apply in that situation because you're not planning on having sixteen drinks. There is no goodwill value in this situation because everyone's taking turns doing it.

Outside of that weird environment, the value of buying a round goes a long way.

Let's say you spot a group of people who are pulling out their credit cards to divide the bill among them. If you pay for all of them, you may end up spending $300, and you might feel like you've been kicked in the teeth a bit.

I've done this before, and I couldn't really afford it. But, when you pay for everyone, it leads to ten times more in business than the cost of that dinner.

If you can afford it, buying a round of dinner is a cool and effective way to offer value, especially for a larger group of people. When everyone starts pulling out their credit cards, instead of giving the waiter more work, you just pay for everything to make it all easier.

I know there are a bunch of apps where people can split up bills, but I personally hate splitting the bill.

I went out to dinner with a friend a few years ago for his birthday, and I've never seen someone eats so much. He ate $200 worth of food while I ate about $10 worth, and he was ready to split the bill 50/50. He drank two full bottles of wine on his own, and it caught me by surprise when he wanted to split the bill evenly.

We all have horror stories about splitting the bill where it's gone wrong. Splitting the bill, even if you're just trying to make sure you pay what you actually own, can lead to a lot of ill will.

Every once in a while, just foot the bill. If dinner is too much, buy a round of drinks. If you're the new person in a group, this will work especially well. People will think you're a really cool person, and it's an easy way to get a bit of goodwill.

It's astounding how well this works, even on the people I'm in business with. I could be at a bar with my business associates, who are all worth $20,000,000. If I buy a round for them, it works astonishingly well.

There might be a level of wealth where this technique won't work. Maybe if someone has inherited billions of dollars, it wouldn't work. But for most of the people I know, it works very well, even if they're significantly wealthy.

You'll find that this works especially well for men. Men often have to pay for their own drinks, and not many people will buy them a round. Even for some women, once they're married or they reach a certain age, people don't buy them a round of drinks anymore. This technique works across genders, age, and in most situations.

You might run into some jerks who are value-takers. This technique won't work on these people, so we don't want to jump in and start throwing money at them. Luckily, these people are rare, and this technique will work for most of the people you are trying to attract.

It's a very simple way of giving someone value. If you can't afford to buy dinner or rent a car for the weekend, spend $20 on a round of drinks for two or three people and start there.

Become an Event Expert

This is the most technical section of this book, but it's arguably one of the most powerful techniques I will give you.

Architecture is one of my passions. Not necessarily in the way buildings are designed, but in the way that people flow through them.

If you understand how a venue is physically designed, you can use that design to your advantage. You can figure out where lines will be the longest and where the bottlenecks are so that you can talk to people who are stuck in a slow-moving area of the building.

In every venue, there are parts of the room where people are moving fast and parts where they're moving slow. If you find yourself at the bottleneck in between, you have an opportunity to strike up a conversation with someone else in the bottleneck.

This technique can be used in any building you're in. Let's say you're going to a conference at a hotel out of town. I recommend getting there a day or two early to memorize the layout of the hotel. Learn the location of the bathrooms, nearby restaurants, and taxi stands. These are the most common things people seek out when they're at a hotel.

If you have this knowledge, it gives you a short-term, incredibly high value. Everyone needs to know where the bathrooms are. It doesn't matter how rich they are; they will need to use it at some point. If you can point it out to them, you become the most valuable person in the room at that moment.

I've started relationships simply because I pointed out to someone where a bathroom was. When they came back, they said thank you, and we struck up a conversation. If someone else points out the bathroom to me, I always make sure to come back, say thank you, and have a short conversation with them, just in case they're using one of my own tactics against me.

When you go to an event, there are always pamphlets with useful information on them, but, most of the time, no one has the time to read it. They're so busy that they don't even worry about where a restaurant is until they get hungry. If you know where everything is, you can be the one to point it out to them when they need it.

You can even go a step further, although this step isn't necessary. You could learn where all the specialty places are.

There are plenty of people who are vegan, lactose intolerant, have a disease, or have lots of allergies. If you know where all the vegan restaurants are, you could easily point it out to a vegan, and they would be incredibly grateful to you.

It can be stressful when you're traveling to an event and trying to find a restaurant that caters to your specific needs. If you are conscious of restaurants that are all-inclusive of the various allergies and preferences that people have, it is both an act of kindness and a valuable piece of knowledge.

You don't necessarily have to go to a location to know about the layout. You could easily look at maps to find nearby restaurants, and you can even use Google street view to see what the restaurant looks like. This way, you can point it out to someone and really sound like you know your way around.

With just a few hours of prep work, you can be fully prepared to be a personal concierge to the people at an event.

You should think of events the same way people plan robberies in the movies. They have outlines and strategies, and they know the traffic pattern. If you get into that mindset and pretend you're planning a heist, it makes this technique fun.

The preparation will pay off. You have a value that doesn't cost you any money by simply being familiar with a location that others are unfamiliar with.

Venue Master

Instead of focusing on the layout of a venue, you can focus on the people that work there. Specifically, you can learn their names and get to know them.[13]

Your mindset should be to talk to everyone who works at a venue, learn their names, learn what their highest value is, and learn something interesting about them. Every time you run into them, you should say hi and bring up a topic that you know they would be interested in.

You can start with the lowest paid employee and work your way up to the very top. When you're at a location where everyone knows you and you know everyone else, you are perceived as incredibly valuable.

I had a friend who thought that the United States citizenship test should be whether or not someone knows every item on the secret menu at Jamba Juice and In-n-Out Burger.

If you didn't know that they have secret menus, then you're on the outside. Once you know a good bit of the items on the secret menu, you're in the inner circle. When people see you ordering off the secret menu, they will think you have an amazing inside connection.

This can also work on a larger scale.

When you meet the staff of a restaurant where an event is going to be held, you can increase your value just by being close to the waitstaff. If you have a question, you can talk to the waiters.

You can even make life easier for everyone by knowing the waitstaff. If you see that someone has a problem with their order, you can say, "I'll go talk to Jenny and take care of this for you."

When you talk to Jenny, you can say, "The steak wasn't cooked right. I know that if he sends it back, you're going to get in trouble. Can we just order a new steak? I'll pay for it so that you don't have to worry about getting in trouble. I know you and the chef are trying your best, and I'm sure it was just a miscommunication."

You might have to pay for a $16 steak, but you're making life easier for everyone involved. What's more, Jenny will always remember you as the person who tipped well, made her job easier, and took a real interest in her life.

As you strengthen your position at a venue, the value you can give grows stronger. You may even be able to get people into things for free or get discounts. It all starts by implementing these simple principles of giving value and treating everyone like they matter.

I have used these four techniques in a dozen countries and half a dozen languages. These are universal techniques. They work for dating, business, and friendship. Helping people with transportation, finding the bathroom, and treating people right are universal values that everyone can appreciate.

At the beginning of this book, I told you that treating people right will pay off. You can see now why that is. Even though you're without intent and you're not treating people right just to get a benefit, you get one. That's the really amazing thing about these techniques.

Reflection Questions

It's time to think about all the different pieces of this book. For these questions, we're going to reflect on this chapter as well as everything we've learned up to this point.

1. Think back to our original concept of being without intent and treating people right. Do you see the value of that mindset? Do you see that there is a payoff when you do good things and plant good seeds in the world?

2. Think about our earlier lessons. We've talked about treating people right, giving people value, learning about fun, and the techniques for strengthening connections with people. Do you see how these come together? Do you see that these can be effective no matter the situation? Do you see how there can be a payoff, even if the person you're talking to doesn't have anything that could help your business? Treating people right might lead to someone else seeing, or they might know someone who could be good for your business.

3. Think about the places you go the most often. It could be a restaurant, a bar, or a movie theater. What percentage of the staff do you know by name? How many of them know your name?

You may have a different type of relationship with the staff of different venues. If you go to the movie theater, you might never have to order candy because the staff already knows what you like. You might have a relationship where you wave at each other or give each other high fives.

I used to go to a bar in London all the time. The staff knew me and knew that I only drank Tequila Sunrise. It was the special the first night I went there, and I just stuck with it. I would hold up one, two, or three fingers, depending on how many friends I was with, and they would automatically make that many Tequila Sunrises.

I developed a relationship with the manager there, but I never spoke to him outside of the bar. We lived in the same neighborhood, and we would wave at each other if we passed on the street, but it was important to both of us that we never actually talked. We had a very specific type of relationship that we wanted to maintain.

Look at the venues you go to frequently and analyze the relationship you have with the staff.

4. If you've ever worked in retail or have heard stories from someone who works in retail, think about that experience. How do you feel about the customers who treat you like a part of the machine? How do you feel about the customers who know your name?

I want you to think about this experience and write a paragraph about it. What does it feel like when one person out of every 100 treats you right? Are you going to remember that person? Are you going to repay them? Are you going to let them know when there's a sale or a coupon they didn't ask about?

Activity

This activity is going to encompass everything we've learned in this book. It's your big action plan.

Throughout this process, you've been practicing in environments where there are no social consequences. You know the steps of the conversational process, and you have set a particular goal.

Maybe you're looking for a romantic relationship, maybe you just want more friends, or maybe you want a promotion, a raise, or a new job. When I move to a new town, I use this process and these principles to find new friends. Whatever your goal is, these techniques will work to help you reach it.

Your next step is to make a plan that you can use within your social environment.

Choose a location or an event within your environment

that will help you reach your goal. Look at the blueprints for the venue and case it just like you would for a robbery.

Look at the structure of the architecture and the nearby places. Where's the nearest restaurant? Where's the nearest taxi rank? Get familiar with the location. The important landmarks will be different for each type of location, so you need to cater this activity to your environment. If it's a music festival, learn the location of the different food trucks. If it's a hotel for a business conference, find restaurants and classy bars nearby.

In your action plan, get specific. You need to have a specific result, a specific type of person you want to me, and a specific way to build up value.

At the start of this book, I mentioned the Facebook group for all of the people who read my books. I'd like you to post your plan in the group. I'll read it and give you feedback to help you develop the perfect plan.

You're part of my tribe now, and the people in my tribe help each other. When you post on the Facebook group, the other members will help you out. We have an incredibly supportive group, and we love to help each other through whichever process we're going through.

After you've posted your action plan in the group, you're going to implement phase one. This is the "before the robbery" where you lay the groundwork. You're going to go to the venue and meet everyone on the staff.

When you form relationships with the staff, you can maximize your advantages. For every social situation you enter, it's worth maximizing your advantages.

Once you have your plan, once you've shared it with me, once you have some feedback from the group, and once you've laid the groundwork, it's time to implement. Go to your venue and use the techniques I've given you to reach your goal.

I am so excited to hear about your massive success when you find the partner of your dreams, as you form the business relationships you deserve, and as you get the raise that we both know is coming your way.

[13] I have covered this strategy extensively in training videos on my website.

14

PRACTICE MAKES PERFECT

This book doesn't teach principles or tools; it teaches skills. You can learn these skills and practice them until you have mastered them.

Until I was seventeen, I had no friends and I was horrifyingly lonely. Everything I know about forming bonds and making connections is learned. Nothing about my personality, the way I talk to people, or the things I do for fun are natural. Everything I know I had to learn and intentionally work on to improve my lot in life.

We are on the same journey. I have been exactly where you are now, and I understand what you're going through.

The way to master this process is through implementation. There are so many great pieces of knowledge in this book, but even the best piece of knowledge won't stick if you don't do your part.

You can't just read through this book and expect all the techniques to work instantly. You have to practice, experiment, and calibrate to tailor these techniques to your personality and your environment.

If you haven't done any of the activities, you haven't

really read this book, and you have to go back to do it if you really want to get anyone to like you. If you don't have a Journal with all your answers to my questions and with your tracked progress, you're going to hit a massive wall.

I've given you the knowledge, and you have access to all the support you might need, but you have to do your part by calibrating and practicing the techniques you have.

The important thing to remember is that, just like swimming, each of these techniques and principles requires practice in the real world.

If you ever need support, you are more than welcome to message me through the Facebook group, and I will personally respond to your questions.

I can't tell you how supportive this Facebook group is. They are always there to give you feedback, and you're encouraged to share your stories and experiences in the group.

It's my turn to ask you a favor. Whether you're reading this on Kindle, reading a paperback edition, or listening to the audiobook, please take the time to click that fifth star for me. Getting positive reviews makes a huge difference in supporting my family, as well as getting the word out there to help people have better lives.

If you've tried the activities and they honestly didn't work for you, you're within your rights to talk about how this book didn't work. If you haven't done any of the activities, and you're tempted to give a bad review, that's not really fair.

This is an instruction manual. The only way to know if an instruction manual works is to try it.

If you get a couch from Ikea, read the instructions on how to put it together, but you never actually build the couch, you don't know if the instructions work. You can't review them because you don't know. The same principle goes for this book.

I want your honest feedback. Not just in a review, but in a personal message. If there was an activity that you tried but couldn't master, reach out to me and let me know. I can help you find a solution so that you can find success.

There may be parts of this book that didn't work perfectly for your situation. If you're trying to form a specific type of relationship, you may need to ask me for help to customize and calibrate the techniques. I'm more than happy to help you with that.

You're a member of my tribe, and I'm invested in your success. You've read something I've written, and you've invested time with me. That means so much to me.

If you email me or message me in the Facebook group, I'll reply. I want to help you find success so we can be in an alliance with each other.

Learning how to make people like me changed my life, and I want to share that knowledge with you. I went from someone with no friends to someone with a massive army of friends, an amazing group of business partners, and a beautiful family.

The happiness and success that I have found is thanks to the techniques I outline in this book. I can tell you from experience that the more you practice each technique, the better you'll get.

We're on this journey together, and I'm excited to see where things take you. I would love to see pictures of you with your new friends or the new boat you buy once you have found some success using these techniques.

I strongly recommend that you join my tribe so you can communicate with other members. You'll be able to network with like-minded people and get advice to help you gain even more success. Having an amazing community is the whole reason why you read this book in the first place.

I'm so excited that you read this entire book. It means a lot to me, and I'm proud to have you as a new member of my tribe.

LET'S SOAR TOGETHER

The hardest part of personal growth is going it alone. This is a book about developing social skills and communicating with other people.

We have put together an amazing group of people on the same journey as you who would LOVE to help you succeed.

Join something bigger than yourself where you can get the support, feedback, and guidance you need to achieve your desired success.

Please join my FREE, private Facebook group, filled with supportive people on the same path.

https://servenomaster.com/community

This is a great place to chat with me daily, share your experiences with the exercises and find a supportive group of people who are all on the same journey as you.

MORE INFORMATION

Throughout this book, I mentioned other books, images, links, and additional content. All of that can be found at:

https://servenomaster.com/likeyou

You don't have to worry about trying to remember any other links or the names of anything mentioned in this book. Just enjoy the journey and focus on taking control of your destiny.

FOUND A TYPO?

While every effort goes into ensuring that this book is flawless, it is inevitable that a mistake or two will slip through the cracks.

If you find an error of any kind in this book, please let me know by visiting:

ServeNoMaster.com/typos

I appreciate you taking the time to notify me. This ensures that future readers never have to experience that awful typo. You are making the world a better place.

ABOUT THE AUTHOR

Born in Los Angeles, raised in Nashville, educated in London, Jonathan Green has spent years wandering the globe as his own boss – but it didn't come without a price. Like most people, he struggled through years of working in a vast, unfeeling bureaucracy.

After the backstabbing and gossip of the university system threw him out of his job, he was devastated – stranded far away from home without a paycheck coming in. Despite having to hang on to survival with his fingernails, he didn't just survive; he thrived.

Today, he says that getting fired with no safety net was the best thing that ever happened to him. Despite the stress, it gave him an opportunity to rebuild and redesign his life.

One year after being on the edge of financial ruin, Jonathan had replaced his job, working as a six-figure SEO consultant. With his Rolodex overflowing with local businesses and their demands getting higher and higher, he knew that he had to take his hands off the wheel.

That's one of the big takeaways from his experience. Lifestyle design can't just be about a job replacing income, because often, you're replicating the stress and misery that comes with that lifestyle too!

Thanks to smart planning and personal discipline, he started from scratch again, with a focus on repeatable, passive income that created lifestyle freedom. He was more successful than he could have possibly expected. He traveled the world, helped friends and family, and moved to an island in the South Pacific.

Now, he's devoted himself to breaking down every hurdle entrepreneurs face at every stage of their progress, from developing mental strength and resilience in the depths of depression and anxiety, to developing financial and business literacy, to building a concrete plan to escape the 9-to-5, all the way down to the nitty-gritty details of teaching what you need to build a business of your own.

In a digital world packed with "experts," there are few people with the experience to tell you how things really work, why they work and what actually works in the online business world.

Jonathan doesn't just have the experience; he has it in a variety of spaces. A bestselling author, a "ghostwriter to the gurus" who commands sky-high rates due to his ability to deliver captivating work in a hurry, and a video producer who helps small businesses share their skills with their communities.

He's also the founder of the Serve No Master podcast, a weekly show focused on financial independence, networking with the world's most influential people, writing epic stuff online and traveling the world for cheap.

Altogether, it makes him one of the most captivating and accomplished people in the lifestyle design world, sharing the best of what he knows with total transparency, as part of a mission to free regular people from the 9-to-5 and live on their own terms.

Learn from his successes and failures and Serve No Master.

Find out more about Jonathan at:
ServeNoMaster.com

BOOKS BY JONATHAN GREEN

Non-Fiction

Serve No Master Series

Serve No Master

Serve No Master (French)

Breaking Orbit

20K a Day

Control Your Fate

BREAKTHROUGH (coming soon)

Habit of Success Series

PROCRASTINATION

Influence and Persuasion

Overcome Depression

Stop Worrying and Anxiety

Love Yourself

Conquer Stress

Law of Attraction

Mindfulness and Meditation Ultimate Guide

Meditation Techniques for Beginners

I'm Not Shy

Coloring Depression Away with Adult Coloring Books

Don't be Quiet

Social Skills

Many Anyone Like You

Develop Good Habits with S.J. Scott

How to Quit Your Smoking Habit

The Weight Loss Habit

Seven Secrets

Seven Networking Secrets for Jobseekers

Biographies

The Fate of my Father

Complex Adult Coloring Books

The Dinosaur Adult Coloring Book

The Dog Adult Coloring Book

The Celtic Adult Coloring Book

The Outer Space Adult Coloring Book

Irreverent Coloring Books

Dragons Are Bastards

Fiction

Gunpowder and Magic

The Outlier (As Drake Blackstone)

ONE LAST THING

Reviews are the lifeblood of any book on Amazon, especially for the independent author. If you would click five stars on your Kindle device or visit this special link at your convenience, that will ensure that I can continue to produce more books. A quick rating or review helps me to support my family, and I deeply appreciate it.

Without stars and reviews, you would never have found this book. Please take just thirty seconds of your time to support an independent author by leaving a rating.

Thank you so much!

To leave a review go to ->

https://servenomaster.com/likereview

Sincerely,
Jonathan Green
ServeNoMaster.com

www.ingramcontent.com/pod-product-compliance
Lightning Source LLC
Chambersburg PA
CBHW031419210526
45464CB00005B/1966